"I love Liz's brave colorful style—it's so refreshing, unexpected, and inspiring. We need more of her in the world, in our homes, so I'm *very* excited to get my hands on this book and stare at all the eye candy."
—**EMILY HENDERSON**, designer and author of *The New Design Rules*

"Liz's work is pure joy—brave, bold, and unapologetically her. I love that this book doesn't hand you rules, it hands you permission: to play, to trust your instincts, to make a home that feels like you. That's the real magic of design, and Liz captures it beautifully here."
—**LEANNE FORD**, interior designer and author of *The Slow Down*

"*Free Style* is an empowering guide to seeing your home, and your own creativity, with fresh eyes. Liz shows how the smallest details, from toe kicks and drawer pulls to lamp plugs, can make a big impact, while also daring us to dream bigger with wall installations and multi-surface murals. She reminds us that design isn't about perfection or trends—it's about play, experimentation, and creating a space that feels deeply, uniquely yours. This book is a spark for anyone ready to embrace their creativity and live more freely at home."
—**JUSTINA BLAKENEY**, artist, designer, and founder of Jungalow

"*Free Style* is truly unlike any other design and decorating book out there—it brilliantly mirrors Liz's personality, her hands-on approach to design, and the aesthetic of her spaces. It's not just a book, it's an experience."
—**BRIAN PATRICK FLYNN**, interior designer and producer

FREE STYLE

FREE STYLE

Unlock Creative Home Designs

Liz Kamarul

WITH ADRIENNE BREAUX
PHOTOGRAPHS BY LIZ KAMARUL

CLARKSON POTTER/PUBLISHERS
NEW YORK

To our sweet dog Cudi, our forever baby. You brought so much joy to our home and will always be missed.

Contents

INTRODUCTION 9

THE SECRET TO BEING A CREATIVE PERSON 18

THE STORIES WE TELL OURSELVES 22

THE WHAT DON'T I LIKE? METHOD 31

THE WHAT CAN I DO WITH THIS? METHOD 77

THE WHAT IF? METHOD 143

MINI METHODS & QUICK TRICKS 191

GET OUT AND GET INSPIRED 215

RESOURCES 236

ACKNOWLEDGMENTS 238

OBEY
WORLDWIDE

introduction

Creativity has always been a vital part of my life.

For as long as I can remember, I've been painting and decorating (and repainting and redecorating) my surroundings, starting with my childhood bedroom.

I grew up in a small town in Northern Idaho, on nearly twenty wooded acres, the only child of two resourceful parents who fostered my imagination, encouraging me to use whatever was at hand to design spaces that reflected my personality. My parents gave me complete creative control over my room, so I developed my decorating muscles at an early age. In the third grade, I came up with the idea to put one continuous shelf along the middle of my walls, around my *entire* bedroom. My dad was happy to bring my design to life, building and installing the wooden shelf I'd imagined. I painted the walls above it a bright sunshine yellow and the walls below a rich crimson red, and for years I used that shelf to display and rearrange little collections of rocks, figurines, drawings, and more.

As I grew older, my bedroom walls became the canvas for my first murals. With little planning, I painted tons of white flowers and green vines across one yellow wall, adding petals and leaves one at a time and watching the mural grow larger organically. After covering that wall with flowers, I moved across to the next canvas—the opposite wall—and painted a forest of tall, thin, white birch trees. I played with color and pattern over and over again, allowing my room to evolve with me as I grew. And I didn't let the walls define where my painting stopped: That birch tree mural extended onto my bedroom's slanted ceiling, making the space feel cozier.

I am so grateful that my parents never told me no when I had a wild idea I wanted to try. I was never worried about breaking "rules." It never even occurred to me that there were any. I internalized early on that experimenting is not only okay but can also lead to cool and unique results.

While I kept my earliest interior designs and wall murals in my bedroom, my parents let me decorate the rest of the house when I entered high school. I started simply and with what we already had: I would restyle the shelves and rearrange the living room a few times a year. I then began painting murals around the house, experimenting with a leaf pattern in the dining room and more nature patterns in other spaces. Using our family home as a playground inspired me to pursue a career in design, and I graduated from the University of Idaho, majoring in fashion and minoring in interior design.

My first real design job was with a home staging company in Portland, Oregon. While I'm grateful for the experience and felt inspired by staging at first, I soon grew bored with the neutral designs. In my mind, home staging seemed to be about removing all the personality from a space and redesigning it in a way that made it appealing to the broadest possible audience. I can understand the necessity of this when you're trying to attract multiple prospective buyers, but it meant that experimenting with color, pattern, and art was not the priority. The goal was to eliminate character, a process that was difficult and discouraging for me. Though I did get to take home one of my favorite furniture pieces of all time—a patterned vintage sofa that I styled and restyled in my own homes for years—because it was too bold for a house we were staging.

Having to neutralize spaces as a home stager made my need to feel creative even stronger, and so I would experiment in the homes I was living in, first a rental and then later, a house in Portland that my husband, Tim, and I were fortunate to buy. Thankfully, Tim is also an art-minded person and embraces all the bold, unique, personalized designs I come up with (and loves to contribute to the creative process).

I took the frustration I felt with home staging and used it to inspire me to see my home as a place where there were no limits on what I could do. Being free to play around with design ideas and not having to follow any rules meant I finally started to feel comfortable and confident again with my own unique style. I tried out any design ideas that came to mind, however weird or unusual, and I didn't worry about what I should or shouldn't be doing. I also got really into thrifting and finding joy in the things that other people get rid of. (And I jokingly started the very long #thisiswhyihavetothriftshopeveryday hashtag.) I began to feel as creative and carefree as I had when I was a kid playing around in my childhood bedroom.

For fun, I started sharing my projects on social media, and something amazing happened. I found (and, over time, helped build) a community of people like me—people who hate having to follow the rules, hate having to meet expectations, and don't want to spend a ton of money on interior design but are looking to create unique and unexpected homes.

After three years in Portland, Tim and I decided we wanted a change. We saved up some money; bought and renovated a 1982 Winnebago Brave RV; got rid of most of our things; packed up our two dogs, Cudi and Bo; and traveled around the United States for six months in search of a new home. We landed in New Orleans, a

Our first home in Portland, Oregon, where I started to find my personal style.

city bursting with color and creativity, where we lived in a rental apartment before buying a converted double shotgun house with three small bedrooms, huge pocket doors, wood flooring, a tiny backyard, and many architectural features. It's here that I've really been able to settle into my most authentic self, taking the time these past eight years to remodel and reshape the house to feel like us. Tim and I have transformed each room with paint, thrift store finds, and DIY projects. And our New Orleans home has come to reflect everything I believe is important about interior design. It's been both a design playground and laboratory.

Throughout my travels, design experiments, and social media posts, I started to find another passion: inspiring others to play, experiment, explore, and break rules—which is why I'm writing this book.

WHAT YOU'LL FIND IN THIS BOOK

My creative process is not formal, and that's a big part of why it's fun and successful. But over the years, I have noticed that a few questions I ask myself over and over help me come up with unique home ideas. In the following chapters, I'll go through these questions one by one, and pair them with real design project photos and explanations. In each chapter, I'll take you through homes I've designed so you can see my mind and my processes at work. You'll be able to follow how I start with an idea (or a thought, or a question) and how it evolves until I end up with a design I like. There will also be space for you to figure out how to make these processes your own and apply them to your home.

Along the way, there will be helpful sidebars about how to reuse or make over things you already have in your home, deep dives into my principles (which begin on page 40), and photos that inspire you to think about your home differently. And I also share tips for taking inspiration from the world around you.

As you read the book, you'll understand the creative method I've honed over the years and find one that sparks your creativity and motivation. By the end of the book, you'll have the tools to transform your home with your own brilliant and creative ideas.

This book will also give you the support, freedom, encouragement, and permission to do what I've always done: make mistakes, use materials in weird ways, and work with what's around, all to create a home that looks and feels like me—not like whatever happens to be trendy right now.

Our dining room in New Orleans.

WHAT YOU'LL BE ABLE TO DO ONCE YOU'VE READ THIS BOOK

After reading *Free Style,* you'll see that there are more possibilities than limitations. That by experimenting and thinking outside the box, you can find your own style, not simply follow whatever style is popular at the moment. Because when you spark inspiration for your home through your own creative experimentation, you won't feel the pressure to change along with the changing tides of design trends. When you design a home that looks and feels like you, and not like the other homes you see online, you'll be less likely to look around in a few months and hate what you see.

When I'm at home, I'm energized. I'm in a good mood. I feel creative. And I genuinely believe it's because I've crafted a space that is fun and filled with experiments and my own ideas. I want your home to make you feel this way, too.

But before we dive in, let me remind you that the very first step is to stop telling yourself you aren't creative.

the secret to being a creative person

A question I'm asked frequently is "How do you come up with your ideas?" After answering, I often hear the same response: "I could never think of that."

But you can.

Even my mom often comments on my work and says, "Oh, you're so creative. I wish I were, too, but I'm just not." Does that sound familiar? Have you ever said something similar?

Here's the truth: There are no limits on what is and isn't creativity. I promise, you *are* a creative person in one way or another.

In my mom's case, I've seen her be creative all my life. But my mom doesn't see it that way. She's told herself that she's not creative so many times, it's become her truth.

You, too, might think you aren't a creative person. You might not know where to even begin to figure out how to *become* creative. This book will help you learn how to tap into your own creativity.

TAKE THE FIRST STEP: ACCEPT THAT YOU ARE CREATIVE

Think about the things you do that maybe aren't *typically* considered creative hobbies but that absolutely involve having to think creatively. In fact, make a list. Here are some thought starters:

- Do you love putting together an interesting outfit that combines colors or patterns in a way that others would consider bold?
- Do you love combining fresh ingredients in a good meal and plating it lovingly for yourself or your family?
- Are you constantly taking affordable grocery store floral bouquets and arranging them at home in your own clever way?

- Do you come up with elaborate or funny themes for parties and events?
- Are you *the* go-to friend when anyone needs a music playlist?
- Do you love to doodle while at meetings, on the phone, or during class?
- Do you know how to stretch a budget like no one else?
- Have you successfully organized your home in a way that works for your whole family?
- Do you love putting together furniture, Legos, model airplane kits, and more?

This list is far from exhaustive; there are so many other ways to be creative that it doesn't touch on. I guarantee there is something about you that makes you creative, even if you didn't see it above. Because creativity isn't about the activity you're doing—it's about how you approach *doing* that activity. It's about how you think about things. It's about not limiting yourself, no matter what it is you're doing, *especially* when it comes to how you decorate your home.

Creativity is everywhere and presents itself in many different ways.

I am so inspired by my fellow creatives and designers, who have come up with so many interesting ideas and creative solutions. I'll share some of those in the book as well.

As you'll see from my projects and the projects of others, fun and interesting designs come from playing around and experimenting with materials, objects, and color until you discover a design you like.

Everyone's creative journey is different. Some people think they never had any creativity to begin with, while others believe they lost theirs along the road of life. Wherever you are on your creative journey, this is the most important thing you can do: Stop telling yourself you aren't a creative person.

the stories we tell ourselves

When designing a home, unless you're a millionaire (and maybe even then, too), you will face limitations that you have to overcome—from not having a big enough home to not having a big enough budget. So why add your own self-limiting narrative on top of that?

In my experience, tapping into your interior design creativity means letting go of negative self-talk and silencing the inner voice that says you're not a creative person or that you can't come up with innovative ideas.

It may *sound* simple, but it is hard. I still catch myself using self-limiting language sometimes. But when I notice negative self-talk, I stop and remember that the best ideas come from letting myself hear "Yes" or "Let's try it!" instead of "That'll never work." The worst thing that can happen from stopping negative self-talk is that you might get the confidence to try a project that doesn't end up working out in the end. The *best* thing that could happen is that you could get the confidence to try a project that ends up being your favorite idea ever.

HERE'S SOME INSIGHT INTO MY CREATIVE PROCESS

I don't let any *shoulds* sneak into my vocabulary when I'm dreaming up decor ideas. I avoid telling myself that there is a certain way something should or should not be done. I don't limit how I can use a paint color, or a pillow, or a building material, or . . . anything. Of course, there are *actual* limitations; safety is essential, and I don't recommend you use any tools unsafely. I'm talking about the times you have an idea (like to paint a part of your home in a bold color) but then tell yourself you shouldn't execute it for some reason. Or a time when you have the notion to use a material in a novel way but then stop yourself, believing that you *should* use things only in the way they are intended to be used.

I'm not guaranteeing that every wild idea you ever have will work out. But how will you know if you don't let yourself experiment?

I believe this is my answer to the question "How do you come up with your ideas?" Because I don't limit the ideas I explore, I end up with many more that I love.

All people tell themselves stories about what they can (or can't) do. And some people tell themselves the story that they'll never be someone who can come up with unique or personal home decor ideas. The danger of not recognizing that these narratives are false is the potential of staying locked into them. You could miss out on something great because you've told yourself that something great wasn't for you.

There are many ways someone can talk themselves out of not only *trying out* a home decor idea but also even letting themselves *think of* an unusual idea in the first place.

Here are examples of stories people tell themselves that may be getting in the way of creating a deeply personal home:

- They're going to be in the home for only a few months, so why bother?
- Their home is not nice enough to spend time or money on.
- They don't have enough money to do what they really want to.
- Their home decor style is minimal so they can't buy any maximalist-style accessories. (Or vice versa.)
- A paint color or wallpaper they like won't go with their home's existing architecture.
- It's against the "rules" to mix certain patterns or colors together.
- They're worried that they won't like the result after spending time on the project.
- They're worried about what their partner will think . . . or their neighbor . . . or their family.
- They're worried about the resale value of the house.
- They think that because they've never tried a certain DIY project before, they aren't capable of doing it.
- The idea is too impractical, or it doesn't make sense to put in the effort.
- They don't want to put a hole in a wall . . . or tear out something . . . or . . .

WHAT
DO
I
DESIRE

WHAT STORIES ARE YOU TELLING YOURSELF?

Stories can be rewritten. Rather than limit yourself before you even start, why not recognize the stories you tell yourself that could be keeping you from having the incredible, creative home of your dreams?

What is the architectural style of your home? Is it a 1970s ranch? A brand-new build? A tiny studio apartment? An industrial loft? Are you telling yourself that you must decorate the inside to match the building's architectural style?

Do you rent your home and have decided that it's not yours and that you should not do anything to make it look or feel better?

What's your favorite medium of art? Do you just love photography prints? Are you a fan of sculptures? Love a painted canvas? By declaring yourself a fan of a particular type of art, could you be blinding yourself to the possibilities of others?

Have you told yourself that there are specific colors that just won't work in your home?

What kind of room in your home do you wish you had the space for? An office? An arts and crafts room? A library? Have you told yourself that you can't find the space in your home for one of your passions because you don't have a dedicated extra room for it?

FORGET ALL THE STORIES YOU'VE TOLD YOURSELF

It doesn't really matter what your home's architectural style is—you don't have to furnish it to match. It doesn't matter if you own or rent your home or if you plan on staying in the space for only six months: You deserve to live in a home you love, and designing it is worth the effort.

If you define your style as exclusively "modern," then you might miss out on incorporating cool design elements because they don't fall into that category. If you tell yourself that you can't buy an ornate table because your other furniture is clean-lined and mid-century, then you could be missing out on a seriously cool combo that would reflect your personality.

Forget all the stories you've told yourself about who you are or what style of home you have. And read on to discover the methods I use to come up with creative home decor ideas. *Not* so you can copy these projects exactly. But so you can retrain your brain to stop limiting itself and to come up with your own decor ideas that will make your home one of a kind.

THE STORY I TOLD MYSELF

For the longest time, I told myself that interior design was all about obeying rules, following trends, and creating those picture-perfect spaces you see everywhere. Spaces that sometimes end up looking more like someone else's idea of a home than your own. But designing your home shouldn't feel like following a checklist or trying to impress anyone else. Creating a space that reflects you—your personality, your quirks, and your life—is the most important design element to get right.

Every project in this book could've been created using *any* of these methods. They're interchangeable and flexible because they're more about sparking ideas than giving you strict instructions. You might already be using some of these methods without realizing it. As you read this book, you'll see examples from my own projects and from other creatives' projects that I believe exemplify these methods, even if the designers didn't use them when they were designing.

The methods aren't groundbreaking inventions. Or rigid techniques that you have to follow precisely. They're just ways to think differently about design. They are simple, nonscientific, and a lot of fun—and I believe they are ways you can encourage yourself to think differently about design. To give yourself permission to step back, reimagine, and try something new. If your creativity feels stuck, these methods are here to nudge it loose. If you're bored with your space, they'll help you see it in a fresh light.

By the end of this book, I hope you'll feel like you have a whole tool kit for designing boldly and fearlessly—whether that means using just one method, using all of them, or even creating your own. And whenever you feel frustrated or uninspired, you can come back to these ideas and find your way forward. Because your home isn't about rules or trends. It's about *you*.

THE WHAT DON'T I LIKE? METHOD

Have you ever felt like one of the rooms in your home isn't finished, but it's not clear what else the space needs? You've arranged the furniture, you've hung a few pieces of art, but something is missing. The room just doesn't look or feel as good as you'd hoped. You're disappointed with the outcome, but you have no idea what to do next. Rather than take on an entire room renovation and start from scratch, you could instead pinpoint one small thing to change. This method is also great if you are in a creative slump, not sure what design direction to go in, or just fresh out of ideas.

The first question to ask yourself is "What don't I like?," and it's one of my favorites because it's so simple. It's about mindfully observing your surroundings, learning how to notice both obvious *and* overlooked elements, and most of all, *not* pressuring yourself.

Anyone can use the "What don't I like?" prompt as a starting point for their next great design idea. And the best part about it is that you can customize it however you like. Play music while you think about it or keep it quiet. Sit in the same spot on your sofa as you always do or sit somewhere unusual, like on the floor, to give yourself a fresh perspective. Write down or sketch your thoughts on paper or just take mental notes.

This method is all about giving yourself a new way to think about your home, design, and even creativity in general. Going through the exercise in this chapter will allow you to think about your home in a different way than you usually do, and that might just be the spark your creativity needs to take off.

These cabinet pulls were made out of scrap wood and painted to match the cupboards for a quick and easy refresh.

ANSEL ADA
GREYSTONE

WHERE TO START

Many of my favorite design projects have started simply: with me sitting in a room of my home and studying the objects and elements within it as if I'm playing a game of "I spy" mixed with meditation. I'm not intentionally seeking the next design project I want to tackle. I'm not even trying to find design inspiration. And I'm certainly not trying to force something beautiful or creative to happen. I'm just mindfully observing all the details of the room, big and small.

The basics of the method are pretty simple. What I do to begin is let my eyes move around the room, briefly resting on different components of the space. The key to success is that I *don't* look around with an agenda. I'm not looking specifically for something to paint, for example. Or for an object I can remove from the room. I'm just looking around at what is currently in my space.

I do try not to let my mind wander as my eyes do; I make observations and take mental notes about what I'm seeing (instead of letting myself wonder what's for dinner). Think of the common meditation practice of closing your eyes and observing how various parts of your body feel; I'm doing the same with my room, noting how things look to me. I don't start this exercise in any one spot, but if you need a place to start, begin at the top of your room with the ceiling and then let your eyes follow details down to the floor.

WHAT TO DO

When I do this exercise, I often start by looking at the furniture in the space. I glance at shelves and surfaces and I also look at accessories and other objects on those surfaces. I examine any art in the room, noting where it's hanging, what the frame looks like, and what surrounds it.

But I'm not simply looking at the pretty or decorative things in my home. I'm going beyond the surface decor and trying to notice the other elements some of us tend to overlook the longer we've lived in a space, like baseboards, moldings, window trim, and other architectural elements that were in the home when we moved in. I look for blemishes on the wall surfaces. I examine installed objects like light fixtures, faucets, and more, evaluating what kind of condition they're in.

Slowly observing my surroundings without any design agenda lets my brain and body notice what in a space bugs me. It helps me pinpoint details that I find boring or ugly or that I might want to change.

When I'm able to identify something in the space that bothers me, I then allow myself to fixate on that one annoying detail or object. The thing that catches my eye doesn't have to be big or splashy. It could be an architectural element that's not my style, like a cabinet knob. It could be something that's damaged or dirty, like a piece of furniture or a pillow. It could be something that's just blank, like a plain bathroom mirror without a frame. It could be something I wish were gone, like window blinds or a lamp cord. It doesn't really matter what *it* is. This exercise is all about finding an *it* in your space that elicits a negative emotion.

Because when I've found something in my space that I think is either ugly, damaged, or not my style—simply put, something I'd like to change—I have the jumping-off point for a creative project.

Once I've discovered an answer to "What don't I like?," I then interrogate myself about *what it is* that I don't like. This can give me even more hints as to what direction I should go in creatively. Let's say the "it" in this example is a cabinet knob that's not my style. I don't just stop at thinking, "I don't like the cabinet knob." I ask myself what it is about it that I don't like. Is it the finish? The shape? Does it feel too small? Too big? I try to narrow down what it is that I don't like about something, because then I can figure out what I want that object or element to be.

In other words, if I don't like an object's finish, I can start thinking about ways to change that finish. If something feels too small, I can start thinking about ways to make it physically bigger or visually more significant. Pinpointing what you don't like about something allows you to determine what you can change.

WHAT NOT TO DO

Again: What I'm not doing (not yet, anyway) is *trying* to come up with any creative decor ideas as I look around the room. I don't like to put that kind of pressure on myself. In fact, telling myself that I must go into a room and come up with a creative idea is the fastest way to give myself a creative block.

GRAFFITI AND URBAN ART
The McCall's Book of Handcrafts
"ANIMATOR'S SURVIVAL KIT
IN THE COMPANY OF WOMEN
THE NEW BOHEMIANS
HOUSE BOOK
Hit the Road
Plant Tribe
100 IDEAS GRAPHIC DESIGN
ALL ABOUT DECORATING

SQUIGGLE CORD

One day I found myself sitting on our sofa, staring at the cord of a wall sconce. I loved the light fixture and where it was located, but the cord was bothering me. I couldn't have the fixture hardwired to hide the cord in the wall because of the adjacent pocket doors, but I also wasn't able to stop being annoyed by the way the cord looked. It just hung there from the sconce, a black line against the wall's cream paint color. And because of the sconce's placement above an armchair, there was no way to hide the cord with a stack of books or some other decor element. The cord looked ugly and messy. And more than that, I felt like it distracted from the other beautiful elements in that corner of the room.

I knew I wanted to do something to change the way the cord looked.

So, as I studied the cord, I let my mind wander, thinking about ways I could make it look different. Could I try to camouflage it by painting it the same color as the wall? I considered it, but I knew I would still be able to tell there was a cord there.

As I reflected on design elements that I was drawn to at the time, squiggle patterns came to mind. I had noticed squiggle patterns in paintings, fabric, and furniture in inspiring rooms I saw on social media and in design books. And it's okay to incorporate a trend in your home if it's something you truly like (see my note on trends on page 72).

Then I had a lightbulb moment: I realized I could marry a shape I was really drawn to (the squiggle) with an object I didn't like (the sconce cord) to create something that looked both innovative and intentional (see page 38).

don't stop at your first idea

The first idea you have about a project can be brilliant. But why not see *just* how clever and creative you can get? One of the most important principles to remember is to not stop at your first idea.

For one, you never know what incredible ideas might be hiding right after your first one. Sometimes my first idea is great. But sometimes, after I take a moment or two to keep thinking, I discover that my original idea could go one step further. In our bedroom, I took the squiggle cord idea and enhanced it by painting a bold red color behind the cord to really make it pop.

Our first ideas tend to be the most obvious ones. Maybe something you've seen before. And while your first idea might be doable, try to push yourself a little further because that's when the creativity really begins.

I'm not suggesting that simple ideas aren't good. As you'll see throughout this book, sometimes the simplest ideas are the most stunning, stylish, and clever. But I *am* advocating for not stopping at that first idea, however simple or complex it may be. Because even if you end up going with your first idea in the end, the exercise of challenging yourself to come up with additional ideas is worth it.

Daring yourself to keep coming up with ideas beyond your first one is a big part of exercising your creativity. The thinking itself is what is creative, and the more you think, explore, and play with what could be possible, the more you open yourself up to even more ideas. You're practicing being creative.

And exploring all the different iterations of an idea before you settle on the best one allows you to *really* end up loving the idea you decide on.

Our bedroom in New Orleans featuring art made by local artist Read More Books.

CANNED CEILING LIGHTS

I decided to color drench our back room by painting the walls and ceiling an olive green. Before, when the ceiling was white, I never even noticed the can lights. But after, they contrasted with the green and stuck out like a sore thumb. First, I considered painting the rims around the lights green as well, but that still left the white lightbulbs clashing with the green. I researched buying covers to close the lights up altogether since I rarely use them anyway, but that felt like a decision I might regret one day. Finally, I realized that instead of fighting with the lights and trying to remove them, I could just work with them. The first thing that popped into my head after looking at the lights and their shape was eyeballs. Specifically, animal eyeballs. That's when a mural felt like the perfect solution. I painted a series of animals and used the lights as their eyes. Now the lights have gone from something I didn't like to part of a fun feature for the ceiling.

TRIANGLE WALL

One of my first decor projects where I had the freedom to do whatever I wanted (and not have to worry about putting sixty nail holes in a rental home's wall) is also a personal favorite. Not just because I love the look of it but because it embodies key principles I value in home projects: using simple materials like plywood and paint and playing around and experimenting.

When Tim and I lived in Portland, I designed a maximalist living room. The space was filled with art, color, accessories, and patterns, except for the wall above the sofa, which felt empty. It was the focus of what I didn't like in the room. I wanted to add visual interest without overwhelming the already busy room, and I didn't want to compete with the gallery wall on the opposite side.

I considered how to add dimension to the surface. With plenty of time but a limited budget, I focused on manipulating materials to create texture. Plywood came to mind because it's easy to cut, paint, and attach, and its thickness would provide just the right amount of depth. Plus, we already had a sheet of it lying around from a previous project.

I decided to cut the plywood into small, equal-sized triangles and arrange them into a geometric pattern on the wall, and I planned to paint both the triangles and the wall in the same color to achieve a subtle effect that would make a statement but not steal too much of the limelight. I carefully laid out the pattern on the floor first, getting it just the way I wanted it. But before I could finish, our dog Bo ran across the triangles I had arranged, "messing up" one corner of the geometric pattern and spreading the pieces out randomly.

Instead of redoing it, I embraced the accident and incorporated Bo's design. The resulting wall featured a unique pattern of black triangles on a black background, with slight visual differences between the wood and wall finishes. Bo's accidental contribution made the design truly one of a kind, and it taught me the value of being open to unexpected changes in the creative process. It's also worth noting that design doesn't need to be perfect. It's okay to just hang up a piece of art without pulling out the measuring tape or to skip using a ruler when you are drawing stripes on a piece of art. There's a time and place to be a perfectionist, but it's also fun to just go with the flow and let the imperfections shine.

vintage couch

Something I'm really passionate about is reusing. Everything from thrifting secondhand furniture, art, and accessories over buying new to recycling existing building materials in fresh ways. Instead of throwing away something in your home you don't love, first try to alter it in a way that fits your style. I think this way of interior design creates a more one-of-a-kind home, and it's also better for your wallet and healthier for the planet.

But I don't stop after just one reuse. In fact, there are lots of projects and objects that I've reworked over and over again. Sometimes I didn't love the first result; other times I was just in the mood for something else. Not only do I advocate not stopping at your first idea, I also advocate not stopping when it comes to how many times you refresh the objects in your home.

One of my favorite items that I redid over and over again was a giant vintage couch that I took home for free from a home staging job years ago because it had too much personality.

The couch was long enough to comfortably accommodate five adults. Its deep cushions allowed you to sink into them, and its tall arms made you feel cocooned when you curled up on it. Though it was heavy and hard to move, it was all worth it the moment you sank into it.

But beyond how comfortable this free vintage couch was, what initially drew me in was its bold 1970s-inspired pattern, energetically intertwining wavy lines in gold, reddish-brown, black, and cream. This striking piece became the focal point of three homes, and we even traveled across the country with it. In no small way, the couch jump-started my career, opening my eyes to the power of unique and imaginative home decor.

But more than that, it also served as one of my first design laboratories, proving how powerful making minor changes to an object can be in not just transforming the way a furniture piece can *look* but also how a whole room can *feel*.

Though I loved the sofa's unique patterned upholstery, I'm still me, and I love to change things from time to time. Over the six years we owned the sofa, I made tweaks that changed the vibe but kept its spirit alive. I'm not a professional upholsterer (nor would I ever have covered up all the '70s-style pattern), but I was delighted to discover how easy it was to change just the seat cushion fabric. For the first refresh, I picked a solid orange velvet fabric, which made the couch feel more subdued. Next, I covered the cushions in a contrasting black-and-white mudcloth-inspired pattern, creating an exciting clash of textures. For a quick refresh, I simply folded a striped blanket over the cushions. Look at your sofa right now. . . . Is there a way you could add a different color or pattern to a part of the sofa without doing an entire reupholstery job? Can you slipcover some cushions? Cover the arms? Is there a way to update it with something you already have?

I didn't *just* use fabric to play around with the sofa. At one point I nailed pieces of unfinished plywood to the sides, changing the feel of the entire piece. I love ideas like these because they are easy and affordable to implement and can also keep you from getting rid of your furniture before you need to.

You don't have to start with a patterned sofa to get creative; these are great ideas to implement if you have a plainer one. Maybe try nailing some fringe to the base or switching out all the back cushions for a different color or pattern. The smaller—and the more unexpected—the details you incorporate, the more one of a kind your home will feel.

WOODEN TRIANGLES

The window in the guest bedroom of our New Orleans house felt too plain, but I didn't want to hang curtains or blinds; I wanted to create something to make the window its own feature in the room. I thought back to a project in our home in Portland: the 3D wall texture I'd created by using small cutout triangles (see page 44).

You don't always have to come up with a fresh, never-before-tried idea when you're hoping to improve a space. You can recycle elements or ideas you've used in other ways and in other places; they will look and feel new to you. So, when it came to the guest bedroom, it occurred to me to play around with similar wooden triangles, this time installing them around the window frame. This made the window itself feel bigger, and adding such a unique detail also made the window and wall feel more prominent in the space. The addition helped balance all the elements in the room, without stealing too much of the show.

CABINET PULLS

When we took on a kitchen renovation in our New Orleans house, I already didn't love our cabinets. No matter what we DIYed in that room, the plain white cabinets really bored me. I've always loved the look of natural wood, but the existing cabinets were in good shape and I would have felt guilty ripping them out. I also didn't want to paint them because that felt like too big a project (anyone who has ever sanded, primed, painted, and reinstalled cabinets knows what I'm talking about).

As I stared at the cabinets, trying to think of a way to update them, my eyes kept landing on the door and drawer pulls: plain silver (not my favorite metallic finish) and too small and boring for my taste.

A way to easily change the look of cabinets is to replace the handles. Since I wasn't about to splurge on all-wood cabinets, I thought about how I could add more natural wood texture to the kitchen. My thinking was that the bigger the door pulls, the more attention they would take away from the plain cabinets *and* the more natural wood I could bring into the room.

I looked online for something that would match my vision, but I couldn't find what I was looking for: extra-long, all-natural wood handles that would be nearly the length of the cabinet doors themselves. The design I came up with was a thin, flat rectangular piece of wood curved at the bottom, which created a space for fingertips. I had my dad build the pulls to my specifications, and then Tim and I screwed them into the cabinet doors. Easy to make, cost-effective, and incredibly dramatic, the new pulls work as intended, deflecting attention from the cabinets, and adding lots of natural wood tones to the room.

FROM TUB TO CANVAS

My friend Joey had recruited me to help with one of the bathrooms in his house in New Jersey. He wanted to make the room feel less traditional, and he had already installed a vintage light fixture, mirror, and towel rack that were in bold primary colors and had cool, postmodern vibes. But those additions weren't enough to counteract the power of the claw-foot tub, which was a huge statement piece in the center of the room and an element he wasn't willing to replace. I often turn to paint as a fun way to add a modern look to something that can't be removed. While some people might be nervous about painting a classic claw-foot tub, Joey and I both knew it could be repainted if he desired a traditional feel in the room again at some point.

Another tub transformation happened in the guest bathroom of Tim's and my New Orleans house. The room had a yellow bathtub, and I hated the color. It just was not for me. The tub wasn't cast iron or classic in any way; it was just a simple fiberglass tub, so I wasn't worried about "ruining" it. I knew I wanted to add more pattern to the room to play with the wallpaper. The tub felt like a natural canvas. I painted a simple, repeating checkerboard pattern using one paint color that matched the room's wallpaper and another that complemented it. Painting is often my go-to when I want to change something I don't like—after all, it's easy and usually affordable. And a benefit of working on a small "canvas" is that you won't need much paint to cover the surface; you could even purchase sample sizes of paint to save money.

DOORJAMBS

The hall in our New Orleans house leads to our office, a guest bathroom, our primary bedroom, a guest bedroom, our laundry room, and our living room. We call it our Hall of Doors. Looking at it from the living room was a bit uninspiring, and with little space to hang artwork, there wasn't much we could consider changing apart from the doors and doorjambs. I didn't want to paint the doors because they are beautiful natural wood (and as I've mentioned in discussing other projects, I love natural wood). However, the door frames were already painted, so repainting them felt like a good opportunity to add color and interest to a hallway full of doors (and keep that beautiful natural wood intact). I chose to paint only the doorjamb—the inner part of the door frame—for a small surprise of color.

PAINTED TRIM

Tim and I put in a tremendous amount of work adding green tile not only to our kitchen's backsplash but also on top of the floating shelves we installed. But even after we thought we had finished the room, there was one thing that kept bugging me: The window trim above our kitchen sink was this stark white contrast to the tiles and wallcovering we'd installed. Every time I looked at that wall, my eye was drawn to the bright white frame. That was not what I wanted the focus of the room to be—I wanted to highlight the tiles and the stripes we'd painted on the wallpaper. So, to "camouflage" the trim and make the window blend more into our design, I painted the trim that butts up against the tile the same color as the tile and the part that touches the wallpaper beige to match. As a result, the window fades away and the tiled floating shelves and backsplash shine. Something to remember is that you can do projects one idea at a time. Try finishing one element, then step back and live with it . . . until the next time you're sitting around doing the "What don't I like?" method!

SKIRTED DETAILS

SKIRTED PENDANT

In our New Orleans dining room, I hung a light fixture that I chose because of how sleek and minimal it is. Long and thin, it was just the modern pendant I had been looking for. However, after we added more color and pattern to the walls and ceiling of the room, the minimal fixture started to feel invisible. It was so simple that it blended in with its surroundings, and I realized I was looking for something that had much more drama. I wanted a statement piece. But I also wanted to work with the existing light fixture since it was already installed.

I was hoping to give the fixture a sculptural or textural shape, but I needed to be thoughtful about the materials I used so as not to add too much weight. To create a different shape, I considered lightweight materials like tissue and paper.* Then I came across some photos of bathroom sinks with fabric added to the bottom—commonly referred to as "skirting." I wondered if I could do that with the light fixture.

I went thrifting in New Orleans and came across an interesting remnant of fabric—a thick, small-print plaid in a colorway somewhere between earthy brown and dark mustard yellow. A few bucks' worth of fabric and a little sewing later, and I had a brand-new-to-me light fixture that provided the exact amount of sculptural drama I was looking for.

---

* An important word of caution if you're already looking around at your own light fixtures; mine has an LED lightbulb, so there's no risk of overheating! Don't try this on a fixture with incandescent bulbs.

SKIRTED ISLAND

Fabric skirting can do more than just add visual interest to a light fixture (see page 60). In a house in Sydney, Australia, I was able to significantly enhance a room by adding a skirt in an unexpected spot.

I was visiting my friend Shezeen and wanted to play around with an idea for her minimalist, modern, all-white kitchen. Shezeen and her husband, Nabeel, were open to a little more color and pattern in the space, but they live in a rental home, so they were limited as to what they could add.

We didn't want to install anything permanent in the space or create any damage by using nails or screws. But we really wanted to add some color. Using a tension rod (so no screws and no damage), we hung fabric under the kitchen island, which instantly added texture, pattern, and color to the all-white space. It's the perfect solution for a rental home, and the fabric can easily be changed out for a quick refresh.

"WHAT DON'T I LIKE?" IN THE WILD: JUSTINA BLAKENEY'S HANDRAIL

Sometimes it's the smallest details that can either really bring a space together or break a space. Artist, designer, and author Justina Blakeney's laundry room went through a gorgeous transformation with warm red paint colors on the walls and cabinetry, as well as an accent wall created using Persian Ikat–patterned peel-and-stick wallpaper. The paper's energetic pattern really steals the show, and installing it took Justina's laundry room to another level. But there was a problem: a handrail on the wallpaper wall that had to stay for safety reasons but really stuck out. The solution? By covering the handrail with the very same peel-and-stick wallpaper, Justina was able to turn an otherwise dull and unaesthetic detail into an unexpected highlight in the room.

dining room bench

Our New Orleans home has a giant wood and glass dining table, which I paired with some rounded vintage wooden chairs on one side. On the other side, I placed a large dining bench from Crate & Barrel. Upholstered in bright white fabric, it's a modern piece with a sculptural shape. Over the years, it's been a perfect candidate for several updates.

But I wasn't in the mood to research how to paint the fabric, and I do not possess the skills needed to "properly" upholster a bench with the kinds of curves and details this one has.

Thankfully, you don't have to be a professional upholsterer to update a piece of upholstered furniture. Look for ways to add fresh fabric to a furniture piece that don't involve totally taking it apart. In the case of the bench, I simply staple different fabrics on the top of the bench seat, which allows me to reinvent the bench repeatedly. Each new fabric choice gives the bench a new personality and the dining room a fresh look. And changing out the fabric is something I can do anytime I'm getting bored with the room again.

YOUR TURN

Take a few minutes to look around a room in your home right now. What bugs you? What don't you like the look of? What do you wish you could change but haven't yet? What sticks out like a sore thumb? What have you already tried—unsuccessfully—to hide or camouflage? Here are some potential problem areas that could be your next project:

- Do you have a plain, frameless mirror in your bathroom that you can't stand?
- Do all your windows have the same standard blinds that came with your home when you moved in?
- What about your hallway? Is it too dark?
- Is there a light fixture somewhere that is too small or not your style? Or do you use only "the big light" and want to create a more interesting lighting setup?
- Have you had the same bedroom set since college?
- Do you have mismatched dining chairs that you wish were more cohesive?
- Do you have a pedestal sink and hate looking at the pipes underneath it?
- Are your baseboards dirty or damaged?
- Have your kitchen cabinets not been updated since the 1980s?
- Did you find a cool furniture piece on the side of the road but don't know what to do with it?
- Do you have art you love but hate the frame? (Or art that needs a frame?)
- Do you have a tabletop you love but hate its legs? (Or table legs you love but a top you hate?)

It can be anything.

Once you've identified an object or an element, ask yourself *what it is you don't like about it*. You can start by considering an object's size. (Is it too big for its space? Or too small in the room?) Then move on to an object's finish or color. (Is there a weird texture? Not enough texture? Is the color too neutral? Is the metallic finish silver when you prefer gold? Is it too shiny?) Also, investigate the quality of its construction and whether it's damaged. (Are there cracks where there shouldn't be? What about holes? Is a pillow's seam crooked? Or does a rug have a worn spot on it?)

If you don't understand specifically what it is you don't like about something from those questions, move on to considering whether it's the object's location that's bugging you. (Maybe a big light fixture is the first thing you see when you walk into a room, instead of your favorite piece of art.) Or investigate whether what you don't like is how that object or element interacts with the other things in the room. (For example, the too-glossy finish of a cabinet drawer pull is distracting you from the cabinet door's beautiful natural wood.)

The answers to questions like the ones above will help guide you in the direction of what adjustment you can make. And since the list of things you can do to change something is long, if you get stuck, just start experimenting. Can you paint the thing? Is there a color, pattern, texture, or material that you've been drawn to that you can apply to it to make it look different? Can you combine an element you don't like with something you do like to make the first one new and better? (Say, for instance, you have a throw blanket you love and an upholstered headboard you hate. Trying stapling the throw blanket over the headboard!)

I think one of the biggest myths in decorating is that you must do big, dramatic projects to make any impact on the look and feel of your home. But all the projects I mentioned in this chapter are small, effort-wise. It's not about the size of the change you make in your home or even the amount of time you spend on making a change. In fact, it's not even how *many* of these details you add to your home (though, the more I incorporate, the more my home feels personal and custom to me). I believe a creative home is one where every detail has been intentionally considered and, if needed, altered to fit your personality.

That's what this whole chapter is about, really: intention. Take the time to look at all the elements of a space and evaluate them based on how they make you feel and whether you like them or not. Then, when you find something you don't like, intentionally change the look of it (even slightly) to match your personality.

a note about trends & social media

Social media is how I found a community of like-minded people who were tired of being told what they could and couldn't do, design-wise. It's where my biggest supporters give me confidence every time I try a new design idea. But there's a downside to social media, too. I worry that it's brainwashing us to follow trends.

I hate the word *trend*. It implies that something popular now will be unpopular in a short amount of time. Every year, I see a new crop of posts and videos on social media telling people about what's in and what's out. I see brands posting videos of "dated" design styles and content aimed to make people feel bad for liking something that someone else has deemed "over."

Whether or not we realize it, social media could be making us feel like our homes have to look a certain way. That our homes must be palatable to everyone. I believe that when you spend a ton of time looking at what other people say is trendy, you internalize the idea that to stand out or be different is not good. Scrolling through social media can make it feel like the worst thing you can do to your home is allow it to feel dated.

But our homes shouldn't reflect what's happening in the trendiest design circles. They shouldn't be time capsules of what's hot today. And they shouldn't all look the same. Our homes should be physical reflections of who we are as individuals. Your home should look like you because it's a place where you can be your most authentic self and recharge. Where you can learn about who you are and what you like.

I worry that through social media, we are being fed the message of what a home has to look like to be acceptable, and that's making all our homes look the same. How can your home feed *your* creativity if your home looks like everyone else's?

But beyond just worrying that every home is going to look the same, I find that following the latest trends is just exhausting. Trends used to last so much longer; now it feels like there's a new trend clamoring for attention every month. It's not financially possible to keep up with what's deemed worthy by the masses, and why would you want to spend your time and energy doing so?

I'm not saying you shouldn't be on social media. Just pay attention to your own personal space and how you feel when you're in it. Forget about the internet audience, the influencers, and the tastemakers. Try not to chase the trends that pop up in your feed; instead, follow your own curiosities. Trend or not, do what *you* love.

But—and this is important—you *can* fill your home with trends if you want to, if it's what *you* like. Because I believe the goal of designing your home should be making a space that is filled with all the things you love so you can be your best self in it. I love checks and always will, whether or not they are popular at any given time, so they will always be in my home.

I hope this book helps you discover your own unique home style and helps you stop feeling constrained by constantly changing design trends. Because buying into only what is trendy at the moment is simply another way of limiting yourself and your options.

Repurposed stair balusters made the perfect handles for these doors in the home of Rachel Luria.

THE WHAT CAN I DO WITH THIS? METHOD

If you've ever struggled to come up with design ideas or felt unsure of where to start, the "What can I do with this?" method will help unlock your creativity. This method will encourage you to see familiar objects in new and imaginative ways, helping you break free from limiting beliefs and transform your home for the better.

By practicing the "What *can* I do with this?" method, you're giving yourself permission to experiment with the materials and objects that surround you. It's not about following a rigid set of rules or thinking just like me. Instead, you follow your imagination and maybe even surprise yourself with clever and original ideas that reflect your personal style. Some of my best ideas come when I'm playing with materials, and maybe yours will, too.

This chapter is about pushing boundaries and allowing your imagination to run wild. It's about learning how to look at a piece of wood, a sheet of metal, or even an old rug and see much more. While shopping for furniture and picking paint colors has its place, this chapter instead focuses on something deeper. The "What *can* I do with this?" method will train you to start seeing the extraordinary in the ordinary and teach you how to transform the mundane into something that's uniquely yours. One of the key takeaways I hope you gain from this chapter is the ability to separate what something *is* from what it looks or feels like. Focus on what it *could* do, rather than what it's intended to do.

WHERE TO START

The "What *can* I do with this?" method begins differently than the book's first method. This method begins with a search. Explore your home for materials you can experiment with—things you already have but may not immediately see as having decorative potential. Dig through your garage, attic, basement, closets, drawers, and even your yard. Check in storage containers and cabinets, and behind doors.

Starting with a material rather than a particular spot in your home comes with a bonus: This shift in focus may help you think about design and decor in a new, innovative way.

I won't be giving you a strict definition of what makes "good" material for this chapter's method, because I don't want to limit your possibilities. But to start somewhere, first consider things like construction and decorating materials—the building blocks that make up projects.

To explain what I mean in a metaphor, consider a bakery, where you might find foods like bread, cakes, and other delicious pastries. Those are key offerings for a bakery, but they're not the ingredients. The ingredients are things like flour, sugar, and butter.

If your home were a bakery, elements like furniture, art, and accessories would be the delicious pastries in this metaphor. But the real "ingredients" of your home are things like plywood, metal, wallpaper, contact paper, and tiles. In this chapter, we'll focus on exploring fresh ways to experiment with these ingredients to create something unique.

Gather objects you've thought about throwing away or didn't think you had a use for—things you *think* you know the purpose of.

Maybe you have leftover wallpaper from a previous home improvement project, or there's some excess plywood after you fixed your deck. Maybe your neighbor has a free pile of tiles after they renovated their home. Did you find a bunch of old marble at an estate sale and haven't found a use for it? That could be perfect. Even unusual objects like plastic shopping bags tucked away in a kitchen cabinet could be a contender. You could find something as big as a few sheets of plywood or as small as a roll of duct tape. You're looking for those things that you've tucked away in a garage or a closet—saving for *just in case*.

foraging for ingredients

This list isn't meant to limit what you consider a material or an object—these are just some ideas to get you started for your "home ingredient" hunt.

- Plywood (any size, any condition)
- Loose bricks
- Natural stones or stone remnants
- Rocks
- Ceramic or porcelain tiles
- Broken vase pieces
- Hardwood flooring planks
- Strips or sheets of leftover vinyl
- Random squares of carpet samples
- Cork tiles
- Wallpaper remnants
- Leftover pieces of wall molding or wainscoting
- Old clothes you no longer wear
- Aluminum foil
- Mirrors
- Yarn
- Leftover outdoor pavers
- Leftover fence posts
- Old light fixtures
- Hardware like knobs and handles that you removed when you upgraded but then never got rid of
- Lampshades
- Shoelaces
- Styrofoam balls and other random bits of craft supplies that you have lying around
- Random squares of fabric samples

WHAT TO DO

The first step is to consider a material's intended purpose, which is usually straightforward (and might even be listed on the packaging). Wallpaper, for instance, is meant to paper a wall. Tiles are most often found installed on walls and floors. Some materials, like plywood or lumber, have varied but expected uses, such as for building things. Similarly, tape is generally used to affix items together.

The *point* of listing a material's intended purpose is to empty your brain of all the "typical" uses for a material. Think of it as making room for more unique uses to come to mind. Once you've gotten all the typical uses out of the way, you can start considering all the other types of purposes a material or object could fulfill.

CONSIDER WHAT THE MATERIAL PHYSICALLY DOES

The purpose of wallpaper is to paper a wall. But what it *does* is cover up something you don't like the look of *and* add color and pattern to a surface. A tile's purpose is to be installed on walls and floors, but what a tile *does* is add texture, color, and waterproofing to different surfaces. Consider even a material with a highly specific purpose like privacy window clings (semitranslucent material you affix to your windows) and translate what those *do:* Turn completely clear smooth surfaces either frosted, patterned, or colored. By separating what a material *actually does* from its manufacturer's purpose, you can then begin to consider where else in your home it could be used to advantage. Is there any surface in your home that you don't love the look of or that you want to add a pattern to? Is there something glass, acrylic, or clear in your home that you wish had more color (but that you still want the light to come through), like a shower or cabinet door?

CONSIDER THE LOCATION WHERE A MATERIAL IS TYPICALLY INSTALLED

Another way to dissect a material is by thinking about where it's usually installed and then finding other locations in your home that have similar characteristics. Wallpaper is usually used on smooth walls. But what are *all* the different types of (relatively smooth) surfaces wallpaper *could* go on other than a wall? Ceilings? Floors? Interior columns? A fireplace mantel? Or think about tiles and where they usually get installed: on floors and walls and other solid surfaces. But again—there are lots of diverse surfaces in a home. What's a smoothish surface that could be tiled but is *not* a floor or a wall? Or consider sewing materials like fringe, lace, and fabric trim, which are usually attached to upholstered furniture and other soft objects like lampshades. But you can glue fabric trim onto something like a table edge just as easily as you can sew it onto a throw pillow.

Identifying the typical location where a material is traditionally installed and breaking that location down into its characteristics will allow you to consider other, nontraditional locations that share these characteristics. This will help you think outside the box and come up with your own creative installation spots.

CONSIDER THE AMOUNT OF MATERIAL YOU HAVE

When working with leftover materials, you might run into the problem of not having much material to work with. Don't let this be a limitation. There are ways you can stretch the amount of material you have to make a large visual impact in your space. One small roll of wallpaper can paper only a small portion of a wall, it's true. But cut that wallpaper into pieces and install it so that it spreads the wallpaper pattern out across an entire wall, and you've found a way to add interest to a much larger swath of space than you initially thought you could. It might sound paradoxical, but consider if the material you have can be cut or divided into smaller pieces that can then be installed in such a way as to take up more space. If you're feeling nervous about cutting up the little bit of material you have, I officially give you permission to start cutting.

The flip side is taking one type of object and multiplying it in such a way that those small objects become one big texture, pattern, or feature. Something tiny, like a thumbtack or a paint swatch, becomes a much larger thing when you get a *ton* of thumbtacks and install them all together to create one texture. If you have a bowl, bucket, or container of *lots* of something small, can you combine them so they become a texture that covers a surface?

CONSIDER A MATERIAL'S FINISH

Yet another way you can reconsider an ordinary material is by allowing its natural finish to shine. Instead of rushing to paint or stain plywood or lumber, for instance, why not allow the wood (and all its imperfections) to be the interesting element instead? If the material you're considering is something people typically cover up, what would *not* covering it up look like in your space? How would it look to celebrate a material's natural qualities, rather than try to make that material look like something else?

The flip side of *that* idea is to cover a material that's *not* normally covered. Unless it's specifically made for it, wallpaper isn't typically painted, especially wallpaper with strong textures like grasscloth. But what if you added something on top of it like paint? Fabric? Hot glue?

CONSIDER WHAT YOU ACTUALLY FEEL LIKE DOING

You can also use your own energy level as a direction about how to experiment with something. Have you never installed wallpaper because you dread the idea of trying to line up patterns? What's something else you could do with that wallpaper—how else could you install it—so you don't have to line anything up? Do you avoid certain materials because you don't have the kinds of tools typically used to install them? What else could you do with that material (safely) to add it to your home without using tools you don't have?

You might be asking yourself, "Why take all these steps? Why consider all these things? Why not just put wallpaper or tiles where they're supposed to go?"

You can absolutely install a given material in a typical location if that's what you want to do. It's *your* home, and it should be filled with things that you love and that bring you happiness so you can be your best, most inspired self.

But allowing yourself to be open to new and interesting uses for common design building blocks is what increases creativity in a home. I believe that these mental exercises strengthen your creative muscles, opening you up to more inspiration and possibilities for having a home that reflects your personality and not anyone else's. If you keep looking at things with the same expectations that you always have, you'll keep ending up with the same results.

This isn't just about coming up with never-before-seen designs, either. Exploring alternate ideas for materials can lead to feelings of pride when you complete a unique project. It can make you feel empowered by problem-solving something difficult. It can give you new skills and confidence when you push through a project failure. It can lead to discovering more about what you like and what you can do.

WHAT NOT TO DO

All the thought starters above work for people who have materials or objects lying around to experiment with. If you came up empty after you combed through all your home's hidden spots, you can still play around with this chapter's method. You'll just have one extra step to take before you begin: Go foraging out in the world.

I advocate *not* buying things you don't need and not spending money when you don't have to. So, make your foraging excursions scouting missions for potential future project ideas. You can intentionally seek out places where building materials are sold—a hardware store, your local ReStore, or a reclaimed building supply store. Grab anything that has potential as a material to play around with—and forage for materials or objects that spark your curiosity. Thrift and vintage stores are also wonderful places to be on the lookout.

But you can look out for potential materials in other places, too. The grocery store. A craft store. A lamp and lighting store. And don't forget to check online sources like Facebook Marketplace, Craigslist, estate sales, and local free groups on Nextdoor and Facebook.

When foraging out in the world, there are two basic approaches you can take. You can slowly walk through store aisles, running through all of this method's thought starters above (considering an unexpected location in which to use a material, the amount of material available, what you feel like doing with the material, etc.) quickly for each material or object you come across. Or you can do this exercise only when an object or material catches your attention. You don't have to know *why* a building material or object has caught your attention.

And whether you're working with a material you had at home or one that you came across elsewhere, don't worry (yet) about how little or how much of it you have. Don't worry yet about how you'll be attaching, adhering, or installing it. While at some point in this process you'll have to consider practical matters like budget and physics, now's not the time to think about those things. Trying to figure out logistics at this early stage of the process will only inhibit your ideas. If you start telling yourself, "That won't work," or "No, that's stupid" while you're gathering materials, you'll limit yourself. In fact, don't really worry about anything yet except finding home ingredients to experiment with.

Also important when you're still gathering materials? Don't try to skip ahead and think about what you will *do* with them. Immediately pressuring yourself to come up with a brilliant idea is the fastest way to block yourself from coming up with *any* ideas. Once you've gathered all your materials, you can move on to the next steps of considering the materials' use, how to apply them, how much you have, and so on.

If while in a store or perusing an online ad you find a material that catches your eye, you consider every element of it, and you come up with a brilliant idea for it, you have two directions you can go in. With common building materials that are abundantly available, you have the option to take a small sample of it home to quite literally play around with. With scarce materials or objects you fear might be snatched up by someone else, use your own discretion about whether you should take them home with you. If you have the budget and a strong idea, I say go for it.

No matter if you've found extra plywood lying around your house or are in the hardware store aisle creatively contemplating PVC pipes, commit to running through all the considerations in this chapter to *really* mull over a material from every angle.

PLASTIC TUBES

Once while visiting our local salvaged building supply store, I noticed a cardboard box full of clear plastic tubes with red caps on each end (probably used to ship things like posters). There were a ton of them, and they were only 50¢ each. I had no idea what I would do with them, but I could see there was potential, so I bought a few armfuls just in case. The tubes sat on the floor of our guest room for weeks, and I would occasionally go in there to think about how they could be used. Could I group them together somehow and make sconces for the wall? Would they be interesting wrapped around a vase or hung in front of a window? There was no rush to figure it out, and I spent time letting the ideas come and go. Eventually, I landed on the idea of turning them into a sculpture/light. I loved the shape of them, and because they were clear it felt like a good opportunity to play with light as well.

CREATIVE SHELVING

When Tim and I worked on the kitchen remodel for our New Orleans house, we added green tile to the backsplash, which was installed in a horizontal stacked brick pattern. We then built thick floating shelves (shelves that have no visible shelf brackets) and installed them on the wall to replace our bulky upper kitchen cabinets and display our dishware.

We considered several different ways to add style to the wood shelves we'd created. Keep their natural wood finish? Stain them? Paint them? But instead, I considered the leftover materials we had lying around. As I looked at the tiles we had just installed on our wall, it occurred to me that they could be installed on the flat, smooth surfaces of the floating shelves, too. By adding the tiles, we visually bulked up the already chunky shelves, making them an even more eye-catching, unique feature in the kitchen. This distinctive tile application also created a seamless transition between the wall and the shelves.

Spirited
Elena Horwich

GRAFFITI AND URBAN ART
JUNGALOW
HOUSE BOOK
Plant Tribe
BOHEMIANS
CREATIVE SPACES
DYNAMIC ANATOMY

Tile isn't the only material I've played around with on floating shelves. Tim and I installed even bigger floating shelves made out of plywood in one corner of our living room to make a feature wall and give me a place to display books and accessories. I had hoped that the shelves would be a nice focal piece for the room, but when I styled them with our things, the whole composition felt kind of unexciting and a bit cluttered. I had already been considering different wallpapers to install behind the shelves to give that wall some texture and make it more of a visual statement, so I took a minute to really consider the material and what I *could* do with it.

Because I felt as if using the paper on the wall alone would be adding another element to the already busy design, I imagined what it would look like to wallpaper the unfinished wood shelves as well as the wall. I realized that doing so would make the wall and the shelves feel like one big, cohesive unit—just the look I was going for. By taking the wallpaper application one step beyond just the walls, I was able to create a huge statement in the living room for little additional work or cost. The shelves themselves became a piece of art along with the objects on them, and the whole wall felt grounded and less cluttered.

marble toe kick

I believe in making do with what you already have. There are countless ways to enhance your home's existing elements—through painting, wallpapering, and more—so ripping out something doesn't need to be your first choice when remodeling. This is especially true if the material in your home is still functional, even if it doesn't suit your taste. Before tearing out perfectly good tiles, flooring, or other elements, ask yourself: "Is there a way to make them fit my personality?" Why add to a landfill if you can achieve your vision in another way?

Of course, sometimes you have to rip something out because it's no longer in good shape. Or because what you want to do with your space simply *can't* be done with the existing elements. If demolishing a part of your home is in the cards, before you toss what you've taken out into a dumpster, take a moment to consider if it can be repurposed. I'm not suggesting you reuse moldy or damaged materials. But for salvageable items that don't fit into your design plan, is there another use for them?

I'll provide a great example. When Tim and I remodeled our kitchen, we had to remove a perfectly good marble backsplash to install the new green tiles. The backsplash material matched our countertops, and we liked it fine, but in order for us to achieve our vision, it had to go.

As with everything I remove, I paused before throwing the backsplash away, thinking about how it might be repurposed. I thought about using it in one of our bathrooms or keeping the scrap pieces for future projects. But as I stood in the dining room, looking back at the kitchen, I noticed something: the toe kick—the small, recessed area at the base of the cabinets—was about the same size as the leftover backsplash.

Most kitchen cabinets have toe kicks, a small notch at the bottom of the lower cabinets that makes room for your feet (or toes) and

allows you to reach across the counter without straining. It's an ergonomic detail that you may have never noticed before. Often finished in the same material and color as the lower cabinets, toe kicks basically blend in and are completely unremarkable. But as I stood there, I realized I could seize the opportunity to add a little bit of interest to an often-overlooked spot.

It was such an easy project to glue the old marble backsplash onto the toe kick, and while it's not the first thing you notice in the kitchen, the marble adds a subtle touch of luxury in an unexpected spot. I believe that a deeply personal home is made richer when there are tiny details you notice the longer you look. Along with all the other updates we've made in the kitchen, the marble toe kicks help make our kitchen truly one of a kind. And best of all? I kept something out of a landfill, which is always a big plus in my book.

Betty Crocker's
COOKBOOK

CHECKERED WALLPAPER

I had a little bit of grasscloth wallpaper left over after Tim and I completed the shelving project in the living room (see page 98). And there was a dining room wall I thought could benefit from the paper's natural texture. The problem was, I didn't have a *ton* of paper left. Not enough to paper the entire wall I was eyeing for the project. So, I started to think about how I could stretch the amount of wallpaper I had.

It didn't have to be the only element on the wall. Could I mix what little wallpaper I had with something else to create a look that felt complete? I thought about how I could cut up or divide the paper to take up more visual space. I thought about papering only the bottom half of the wall. I thought about taking the leftover strips of wallpaper and using them like giant stripes on the wall. . . . A possibility, but I wasn't quite sure I'd have enough for more than four or five stripes.

It occurred to me that if I cut the remaining wallpaper into individual, equally sized squares, I'd probably have enough to create a checkerboard pattern that stretched across the entire wall. Combining the grasscloth with another material—the painted wall as the background—would also help me stretch the material I did have.

Though it was a bit tedious to glue each wallpaper square to the wall, I love the result. There's the smallest bit of dimension between the glued-on paper squares and the painted wall squares. The project elevates the idea of wallpaper patterns and takes the whole room to another level.

WALL HANGING

Many of the projects in this chapter involve traditional building materials. But I don't want you to ignore the other possibilities that may be hiding around your home. Just about anything can become a part of something bigger if you keep your mind open.

A fitting example of this is an art piece I created for our New Orleans rental apartment. It combines various elements intended for other uses, resulting in a one-of-a-kind wall hanging.

This project started with three objects I had already: a throw pillow, a small rug, and a grass skirt. Instead of simply moving the throw pillow to a new location when I was tired of where I had it, I separated its use—as a throw pillow—from its texture. Similarly, I viewed the grass skirt, which I had thrifted long ago, not as something to wear but as another interesting texture.

The small rug became the foundation of the project when I noticed how beautifully all three of the objects' textures and colors complemented one another. I played around by layering the objects and swapping them until I settled on a composition that felt right. Then I hand-sewed the items together and attached the combined piece to a branch.

I tied some inexpensive yarn in complementary colors to both sides to complete the look and hung the finished piece on the wall above a rough-hewn wood console table. Guests often complimented the expensive-looking art piece and were amazed when I told them it was made from inexpensive items I already had at home.

So, what components of potential future art pieces might be lying around your home?

"WHAT CAN I DO WITH THIS?" IN THE WILD: JUDY ALDRIDGE'S CREATIVE CARDBOARD ART

It's so inspiring to see what people can come up with using common materials they have on hand in unexpected ways. Particularly when the items are things that most of us just throw away. Instead of tossing out everyday materials like cardboard and newspaper, designer Judy Aldridge instead transforms them into lightweight, fun, and whimsical frames and artwork. Using cardboard as a base, she bunches up old newspaper, forming it into organic shapes with masking tape. Next, she uses a flour and water mixture to add a few layers of papier-mâché to create the hardened final shape. Lastly, a layer of gesso and some paint finish her creations with color and pattern. With the incredibly common (and maybe even free) materials you might already have on hand, there's no limit to the number of unique frames and artwork you can make. How else could you take this idea and translate it for your home? If you don't need frames for your artwork, what about small trays or boxes? Could you transform a piece of furniture using these materials? Are there other similarly overlooked materials in your home you could play with like Judy does?

don't pressure yourself

We're all different people, driven by different motivations, inspirations, and pressures. But if you're anything like me, feeling pressured to create something unique and beautiful is the fastest way to get creatively blocked. When was the last time feeling pressured helped you generate a great idea? For me, it rarely works that way.

Sometimes I feel pressured to keep up with other designers, especially when I'm mindlessly scrolling through social media. And of course, like many others, I also put plenty of pressure on myself. Am I coming up with creative *enough* ideas? Are my ideas good at all? Is it even worth the energy or effort to try them out? At low points, I worry that I'll run out of ideas altogether and will pressure myself to keep coming up with more to make sure I don't.

This pressure—whether from external sources or from within—causes stress. And when I feel stressed, my perspective narrows and my ability to imagine shrinks. I find myself focusing on what could go wrong instead of what could go right.

For me, stress and pressure go hand in hand with fear. And when fear takes the lead, all of a sudden, the stakes feel too high. I find myself dismissing ideas (and even hints of ideas) before they've had a chance to turn into something brilliant. Exploring unconventional ideas becomes out of the question.

I don't claim to know *the* solution to banishing stress, fear, and pressure from your life, but I do advocate for experimenting with ideas, materials, and more—treating it as play rather than a task. When you play, the stakes are low, but the possibility of being delighted is high.

This approach is also why I regularly walk through the methods in this book myself. It's why I don't try to go straight from "I don't like this" to "What brilliant thing can I do?" It's why I don't grab a random material in a hardware store and force myself to come up with a creative use for it on the spot. It's just too much pressure to try to jump straight to the result. I focus on the steps in between—questioning what I do and don't love about something, considering every angle. This takes the pressure off. In a way, these methods are like following clues (and your curiosity) until you sort of sneak up on an idea.

And once you have an idea, you don't pressure yourself to make it perfect—you keep playing, considering, and exploring. You'll know you've hit on something truly good when you step back and can't stop smiling.

Decorating your home should be enjoyable, not stressful. By embracing playfulness instead of pressure, you can let your creativity flourish naturally.

Of course, this is all easier said than done. All you can really do is try to notice when you're pressuring yourself. And if you recognize a feeling of pressure, stress, or fear, pause, remember to follow your curiosity, and just play.

WINDOW CLINGS

Tim and I have installed frosted privacy window clings on some of our windows in the past, and it is a material that I always thought was underused in general. When you think about it, your windows are like potential canvases that could add pattern or color to a room. But of course, many of us don't want to reduce the natural light in our homes, so any treatments you add to your windows have to let it through.

As I explored assorted colors and patterns of window clings, I couldn't help but think of the beautiful mosaic and stained glass windows I've always admired in cathedrals and older homes. I wanted to experiment with this material in a way that mimicked or paid homage to stained glass.

Eventually, the perfect spot to experiment with presented itself. The walk-in shower in my friends Joey and Mark's house has a door to the outside, which we all agree is an amazing architectural feature. This was an ideal place to play around with window clings as they weren't too worried about adding privacy because there were no views to neighbors. The sunlight streamed through these windows, and I was excited to see how the colorful window clings looked.

I experimented with different shapes, textures, and colors, arranging and rearranging the colored films and cutting various shapes of my own as well. Not quite loving the first iteration, I kept going, eventually starting to layer different-colored clings over one another. Because the clings are translucent, layering them created new colors, adding depth to the design. The overlapping layers also formed additional shapes. In the end, combining simple colored window clings transformed the glass door into a glowing, modern, abstract art piece that stands out in the all-tile shower space. An unexpected bonus? As sunlight filters through the window clings, it casts evolving compositions of colorful shadows, creating new, dynamic art throughout the day.

WOOD IDEAS

I frequently use basic lumber in my home decor because things like plywood and two-by-sixes are relatively affordable and widely available. I either already have some extra wood lying around, or acquiring it is as easy as taking a trip to the local hardware store. And just as often, I leave these wood products in their unfinished state. Growing up on my parents' land, I loved seeing all the raw-wood projects my parents incorporated into our home. Wood doesn't have to be an expensive variety to impart natural beauty and warmth to your home. And while Tim and I have some tools that can cut wood, many hardware stores offer basic cutting options for customers, too. To me, using these unassuming materials in fresh ways adds an unexpected element to any room or project—immediately giving your home one-of-a-kind vibes.

WOODEN BEAMS

Our first home in Portland was my experimental playground. It was truly the first place I could play around with whatever ideas I had without a landlord telling me no. At one point, Tim and I built a small wood garden structure in our backyard and had several two-by-sixes left over. We ended up using some of them to build Tim a simple standing desk for the office nook in the house.

The nook was the perfect size for Tim's workspace, but it lacked any architectural character at all. As I considered what else we could do with the leftover wood (perhaps build another piece of furniture?), I really considered the humble lumber pieces. Even cheap two-by-sixes have a natural wood finish that adds warmth to any room they're in. And as I stared at them, they reminded me of the exposed ceiling rafters you sometimes see in houses with vaulted ceilings.

Our little office nook didn't have a vaulted ceiling, and two-by-sixes aren't typically used as ceiling rafters. But I knew that if they were installed intentionally, they could transcend their basic material status. So, we installed seven planks across the office nook ceiling, attaching them to either side of the walls a few inches *lower* than the actual ceiling (instead of attaching them flush to the ceiling). Even though the beams are only six inches wide, installing them a few inches lower than the ceiling made them seem much larger and more imposing than they are. Together, the simple, unfinished two-by-sixes mimicked the look of expensive ceiling beams, adding architectural character to what was just a simple nook.

WOODEN STRIPES AND SQUARES

In our NOLA rental home, I used extra-thin—so thin you could cut them with a knife—strips of wood attached to the living room walls with only an inch or so between, each strip meeting and continuing to the adjacent wall at the corner. The result was very thick stripes of wood that made for a much cooler corner than just painting stripes would have done. And then in the NOLA house that we bought, I used wood from a free and unexpected source—a used shipping pallet—to create another checkerboard pattern in our home, this time in our bathroom. I cut the wood pallet carefully into two-by-two-inch squares that were all about half an inch thick. I nailed the squares onto the wall, alternating wood and wall. The finished project adds more texture than any wallpaper could.

WOOD AS AN UPGRADE

My childhood bathroom in my parents' Idaho house still had all the original '90s finishes: old flooring, a cheap countertop, a simple frameless wall mirror, and a dated light fixture (exposed lightbulbs in a row on a brass base). Since our budget for a refresh was very small, I challenged myself to keep what I could by trying to camouflage certain elements and to replace others with affordable materials that would give the room an upgrade. That's when my thoughts turned to plywood. I love it because it's relatively affordable and has such a variety of uses. With just one piece, I was able to both add a frame to the mirror and cover the dated light fixture (we cut holes for the lightbulbs, so there's still plenty of light). We cut out an irregular-shaped opening and painted maroon and red stripes on the wooden frame that we installed on top of the existing mirror.

The bathroom counter was something that I felt needed to be replaced, but I didn't want to break the bank; even a remnant piece of stone can be quite expensive. Since we had already used wood for the mirror, I decided to continue the theme. We cut a new counter from a thick piece of pine plywood and coated it with several layers of polyurethane to protect it from water.

Wavy wood accents

After cutting out a wavy design for a mirror (see page 120), I was left with an offcut of the same shape. Not one to throw away a perfectly good piece of wood, I went into our RV–which we were in the midst of renovating—looking for a place to use it. I realized it could function as a perfect transition from the ceiling wallpaper to the wall in the bedroom corner of the RV, and it went from being a leftover scrap from one project to the perfect solution in another space.

FRINGE ACCENT

Sometimes when I'm out thrifting or at an estate sale, I'll pick up scraps of "home ingredients" if they appeal to me or are priced well, which is how I ended up with a few yards of white fringe trim a few inches tall and with a white braided top edge. I snapped it up before making a plan for it. Later, back at home, I found myself thinking of ways I could use the fringe in my Portland house.

I looked around at all the soft things in our home like throw pillows, floor cushions, curtains, and lampshades—the kinds of things you traditionally see fringe sewn onto. But I didn't see any soft spots in our home that felt right for the fringe. I wondered if we could take soft surfaces and sewing totally out of the equation. . . . After all, I could also glue fringe onto hard surfaces.

With that in mind, I glanced at our dining table. It was a round white tulip-style table from IKEA, nestled among hand-painted flamingo wallpaper, a colorful patterned upholstered bench, and three dining chairs, each with a distinct fabric seat. Everything in that room was already covered in pattern or fabric except for the table, so I figured why not give it something extra and make it unique?

The fringe trim added to the table's edge immediately looked like it was supposed to be there, thanks to both objects being white. And the fringe's contribution to the table was evident immediately, too: The table became just as playful as the rest of the room.

"WHAT CAN I DO WITH THIS?" IN THE WILD: AMANDA WALKER'S STYLISH STYROFOAM ART

Designer Amanda Walker created a showstopping piece of art that fits her taste perfectly. A fan of textured art, she decided to DIY her own creation. Using a store-bought canvas as the base, she cut and glued lightweight Styrofoam ball halves to it in a grid pattern. Next, she used a premixed joint compound to apply an interesting texture. Adding color with paint and creating a simple wooden frame for the canvas completed the piece. It is not only an unexpected visual result; it's a custom creation that's exactly what she wanted for the room, making her home even more unique to her personality.

TUBE FRAME

During a recent trip to the hardware store for another project's supplies, I took a few extra minutes to follow my curiosity and explore the aisles. Eventually, an unusual texture caught my eye: black plastic irrigation tubing, about four inches in diameter. Its corrugated texture resembled a ribbed pattern or 3D stripes, and I was immediately drawn to how lightweight and flexible it was.

I wanted to incorporate the corrugated surface into my home in some way as a decor item, and as I stood in the hardware store aisle playing with the material in my hands, I saw how easy it was to coil the tubing into a circular shape. Holding the tubing together in a circle, I realized that with little effort, the tubing could be turned into an oversized frame for a mirror or piece of art.

I took a bit of tubing back home with me and glued the ends together. Then, I spray-painted the whole rounded tube shape an earthy taupe color. Those two small steps alone already made the material look totally unrecognizable as mere tubing for water. Using leftover wood, I painted a simple modern art piece (I could just as easily have used some thrift store art) and then screwed the wood to the back of the tubing-turned-frame. The painted tubing, divorced from its original purpose (drainage), has a new life as an art frame.

Tube art hung in home of Joey Meyers and Mark Baehser.

PVC FRAME

Because of how well the tube art frame project came out, I was curious about how I could play with other similarly affordable and abundant materials. PVC pipe is available at nearly every hardware store and comes in all types of lengths and diameters. Along with straight PVC pipe material itself, there are also a lot of differently shaped PVC connectors for connecting pipes to each other. This kind of material has a lot of possibilities for all sorts of home decor ideas. I immediately thought about creating another large-scale art frame. Using PVC pipe and corner connectors, Tim and I built a large rectangular frame. But this time, instead of painting it, I wrapped it in a layer of patterned fabric I found at ricRACK, a great sewing material salvage thrift store in New Orleans. I printed out a photo I took in Morocco in black and white and large enough to fit the frame. You'd never know from seeing it hanging on the checkered wallpaper in our dining room that this photo's frame is made from a simple hardware material.

METAL GATE ART

I always keep my eyes open for one-of-a-kind materials that could be used for surprising home decor, and I had picture frames on my mind after the previous projects. When I found this huge vintage metal gate at a local reclaimed building supply store, I immediately knew it had potential as a frame that could be as much of a stunning statement piece as the art itself. I loved the weathered patina of the metal and knew that the material would contrast beautifully with a lot of different types of art. Unlike with the PVC frame, I love the way the gate's material itself looks; no need to try to cover it. I created a blank canvas by installing a large panel of wood within the gate's frame. And I love how sustainable creating a new use for this old item is.

Artwork hung in the home of Rachel Luria.

"WHAT *CAN* I DO WITH THIS?" IN THE WILD: ROSIE CASE'S WALL SCULPTURE

While shopping at Lowe's one day, design-obsessed writer Rosie Case spotted this staircase riser and knew it had the potential to be something more. Her husband used a saw to cut out a compelling shape. Rosie spray-painted the whole thing a dark gray, and they hung it on the wall. What started out as material intended for an entirely other use was transformed (relatively simply) into a very chic, one-of-a-kind art piece. What items at your local hardware store are just waiting to be customized and turned into art for your home? Or perhaps you already have something around your home you could take a saw and spray paint to? Give yourself permission to see the potential art piece in something common. Anything can be art if you display it with intention in your home.

YOUR TURN

My favorite thing about the projects in this chapter is just how affordable they are. You can create a beautiful home without spending a ton of money, and using basic materials in an imaginative way is part of how I do it.

Rather than start with someplace in your home that you don't like the look of, try to kick-start your own unique home project by considering the material's perspective first.

Take some time and go on a foraging mission right now. I say start anywhere you may have stashed leftover materials from a previous home decor project if you've tackled any recently. You might have a few rolls of wallpaper tucked in the corner of a closet. If you've had any home renovation projects that involved basic building materials, go check out the piles of leftover tiles, drywall, bricks, stone, and more. Is there anything left over that you could consider?

Don't overlook less obvious materials like craft supplies or sewing supplies, and gather anything that could be considered for a bigger and better home decor project.

Do you have a "to donate" box in your vehicle's trunk or beside the front door? Raid it for any possible materials or objects you could play with or experiment with. And remember that objects you no longer love *could* be deconstructed and turned back into their material parts. Old clothes are just fabric. Damaged books are made up of individual paper pages. Old wooden furniture can be turned into scrap wood.

Do you have any friends or family members who have recently renovated something in their home? Give them a call to ask if there are any leftover building materials you can poke through. . . . Most people are happy to have someone take extra things off their hands.

Dig through your kids' old school supplies they're no longer using, or look through your own craft supplies to see if there are lots of small objects you can play around with to make a larger whole. Or find something large, like old posters, which you can cut up, then experiment with the pieces.

While I'm giving you examples to try to spark your own ideas, don't let these be limitations. The list of what could be a home "ingredient" is quite long (see page 82). When you're foraging for materials and objects, try to tell yourself, "Hmm, maybe . . ." instead of "This won't work."

Try to gather materials and objects that are not based on what you think you can do with something (that's skipping way too far ahead in this process). Rather, search for materials and objects based on color, finish, texture, abundance, and other physical attributes that might spark your interest. Let your curiosity guide you to unconventional materials that you want to play with (after considering every thought starter in the "What *can* I do with this?" method, of course).

Don't skip ahead >>> I've said it before, but I'm saying it again because the temptation to figure out what to do with something *before* the process is over will be strong. It may be human nature to think through options and try to formulate a plan. But pressuring yourself to come up with a brilliant idea for a material is skipping over many, many important steps . . . and it may cause you to miss out on great ideas.

Don't get discouraged if things don't immediately look amazing >>> You're embarking on a journey of trying to do things with a material or object that may have never been done before. There are going to be moments of uncertainty, experimentation, and, yes, sometimes even failure. But don't get discouraged; keep playing. When I was working on the wall-hanging project I described earlier, I did *a lot* of rearranging of the layers before I hit on something that I felt looked good. In fact, there were times in the process when I wondered if what I was doing was going to work. But I kept playing around until I found something I liked and was so glad I didn't give up.

Don't make it too complicated >>> Most of the projects in this chapter were done with a nail or a little bit of glue. When you finally do get an idea and then must tackle the task of figuring out how to install something, don't overcomplicate things. Consider the fastest/easiest way to attach your material to whatever surface you'd like it to go on, and try it. You aren't a professional contractor, and no one has to know whether something is "properly" installed. If you're not ruining your home or the material or risking your safety, I always vote for trying the least complicated installation process first. If it doesn't work or stay on, try again! If you have kids or live in a location prone to earthquakes, you may have to make more concessions to ensure that whatever you come up with stays where you put it, but if you don't have to consider earthquakes or kids, try an easy way first.

FEVER

THE WHAT IF? METHOD

This chapter is all about training your mind to go above and beyond your initial thoughts and ideas. To challenge yourself to come up with concepts that are not like anything anyone else has done and that represent you completely and thoroughly. To really play with your home. It's about encouraging yourself to let your imagination run as wild as you'd like it to. Not just for the sake of being different, but for the sake of being your most authentic self. This is how you'll create a home that looks like no one but you. And I believe it's how you'll have the most fun designing your home, too.

Consider the "What if?" method as something similar to improvisational theater (also known as improv comedy or just improv), the art form where performers create without planning or scripting anything—from the dialogue to the plot to the jokes. One of the most basic principles of improv is the idea of "Yes, and," where no matter what one of your fellow performers says, you accept it and then add on to the premise. In other words, if two performers walk out onstage and Performer One starts talking about how it's a beautiful day at the park, Performer Two accepts the idea that they are pretending to be at the park and then adds on to the idea, perhaps by making up something about watching people playing soccer.

The "What if?" method is all about "Yes, and"ing yourself and your own ideas. It's about *not* cutting down your own brilliant ideas before your home has reached its best, most "you" version of itself.

This method encourages you to accept whatever brilliant but unconventional ideas come into your head first, and it also asks you to practice developing your ideas. You start with one thought, but then you let it evolve. You follow small details or inspirations wherever they may lead. Maybe a new idea that is connected to your original one will pop up but in a slightly different way. Just like in improv, the best outcomes happen when you say yes and then build on the original concept by adding personality and flair. Design gets really fun and interesting when you start improvising in your home, but I think it's when you actually start telling yourself yes that your home starts to feel truly unique. The "What if?" method just might lead you to designs you'd never have imagined otherwise.

Another essential element of this method is celebrating even the smallest of changes. In fact, it's the small, overlooked elements of a room, furniture piece, or accessory that are really the nuts and bolts of this method. Details like a rug placed in an unconventional spot (see page 170), a furniture piece used in an unexpected way (see page 186), or paint on a surprising surface (see page 154) can take your home from ordinary to extraordinary. These small details can seem almost unimportant when you're considering them, but they add up to create a home that feels layered, thoughtful, and utterly unique.

Remember, too, that focusing on tweaking small details is an easier way to ease into being bold than doing something huge, drastic, or dramatic. And it can be more affordable as well. The tiny adjustments you make after asking yourself a series of "What if?" questions might seem small, but if you want to know the secret of how a room gets to the next level, it's in the details.

The most important thing to remember when attempting the "What if?" game is to let your thoughts flow without judgment. (And tell yourself yes!)

WHERE TO START

The best part of this method is that you can start almost anywhere, with nearly anything. This chapter is all about training your mind to go above and beyond your initial thoughts and ideas. How can you do something in your home that is beyond what is expected? Are you "yes, and"ing yourself and your ideas? Start with a small project you're already working on or a big project that you think you've completed. You can start with a pillow, chair, fireplace, wall, dresser, or bath towel. You can start underneath a table, above your bed, in a window. You can start with anything in your home that feels like it could be . . . more than it is.

Then, once you've found something in your home—again, it literally could be anything—that you think you could take a little further in terms of pushing its design, ask yourself the question "What if . . . ?" and let whatever comes into your mind be the first thing you consider. It could be something wild, impractical, or even weird. It could be something boring, impossible, or brilliant. It doesn't really matter what it is—just practice letting things pop into your head, say yes, and see where your own brilliant boldness takes you.

Your goal is to genuinely let your mind go a little wild and think outside the box; I'm giving you permission to explore ideas and not judge yourself or anything you come up with. Your goal *isn't* to try to land on the "perfect" solution immediately. Instead, you're practicing opening up your imagination to design possibilities that you wouldn't usually let yourself think of. By asking yourself "What if . . . ?" and then letting whatever comes into your mind be a thought sparker, you might find that one of those wild "What if?"s could be the base for something really amazing.

The beauty of the "What if?" method is in its simplicity. It's *not* a practice where you try to think of great ideas (which can often lead to zero ideas). Instead, it's about letting your mind wander and then following it where it leads.

The main question I'm talking about asking yourself is "What if . . . ?," but there are lots of possibilities for what could come after that phrase. *What if . . . I did this differently? What if . . . this became something else entirely? What if . . . I pushed this idea a little further? What if . . . I moved this ________ over just a few inches? What if . . . I turned something upside down?* Try thinking of the wildest idea you could possibly execute and mull it over. You might realize it's not that wild or out of the question to try.

The questions your mind comes up with don't need to be groundbreaking. What matters is the *process* of playing and brainstorming and exploring whatever you come up with. Every new "What if?" question you ask yourself is like a tiny door to possibility that you open. You don't have to walk through every door, but the more doors you create, the more opportunities you make for yourself and your home project.

WHAT TO DO

Once you've landed on some element or object in your home that you want to play around with, ask yourself, "What if . . . ?," and then just say aloud the first few things you think of. For example, let's say you found a new-to-you dining table. You moved it into your dining room, but you find yourself disappointed with the way it looks in the room. Ask yourself, "What if . . . ?" and let yourself consider whatever pops into your head first.

What if I painted the legs? What if I painted a pattern on the legs? What if I painted the whole table? What if I painted the top one pattern and the legs a different pattern?

Or let's say you don't love how your old, dated fridge looks in your kitchen. Instead of sitting there and trying to figure out what you *should* do with it (like buy a new one), consider instead what you *could* do with it by asking yourself, "What if . . . ?"

What if I got a new handle for the fridge? What if I wallpapered the whole thing? What if I painted it? What if I made a cabinet to hide it?

You can let the "What if" questions flow for as long as you want . . . until your mind comes up with something that sparks your curiosity or gets your heart rate up.

Again, there are no right or wrong answers. You're not trying to come up with a genius idea; you're just following your curiosity to see where it leads. By letting each thought that pops up inspire another thought, without any judgment or pressure, you might just stumble upon a delightful idea that changes your home for the better.

ANSEL ADAMS · THE PRINT

WHAT NOT TO DO

The "What if?" method might feel difficult or unnatural at first, especially if you're used to second-guessing yourself or focusing only on "safe" choices. For some, asking the question "What if . . . ?" can actually feel quite unpleasant because you might be used to filling in the blank with negative thoughts. *What if . . . it doesn't work out? What if . . . I ruin it? What if . . . people think it's stupid?*

If you've been in the habit of telling yourself no, you may have to practice telling yourself yes. Because you are essentially telling yourself no when you fill in the blank after "What if?" with negative thoughts.

When you allow yourself to answer "What if . . . ?" with something positive instead of negative, you give your mind permission to think without constraints. You're allowing unfiltered design ideas from the hidden parts of your mind to surface. So, as your mind fills in the blank after you ask it, "What if . . . ?," it's important that you try not to judge or censor your ideas; even if an idea seems a little impractical, let it exist. Mull it over. Don't immediately shut yourself down. Don't get in your own way. Have fun, and your home will reflect that.

I believe that creativity is most active when there's freedom to play, so keep your mind open and your judgments out of whatever it is that enters your head. Let one idea lead to another without thinking about whether something is doable or even a "good" idea or a "bad" idea. Your first idea might not be "the one," but that's okay.

Consider every new idea that pops up as simply a step in the design process rather than a final destination, if that helps take the pressure off. You're just exploring ideas. You're not committing to anything. Every idea you allow to exist is simply a new opportunity to explore and play. The phrase "What if . . . ?" can be empowering or paralyzing, depending on your mindset. To make the most of this method:

- Focus on positive possibilities. Instead of thinking, *What if I mess this up?,* try reframing it as: *What if this turns out amazing?*
- Stay practical but open. While it's important to respect safety and structural integrity, don't let fear of failure stop you from experimenting.
- Remember that no tweak is too small. So, if you wonder whether something might look better if you moved it a foot or two, try it!

- Switch up the questions to help inspire different ideas. While the method is called "What if?," there are other questions you can ask yourself that might help spark ideas. I personally also love "Why not?" and "What would be a fun thing to try?" I've used all three of these thought-provoking questions to help me shake up details and come up with fun ideas.
- Remember that there are no rules when it comes to objects, so feel free to ask where else an object could live and what else it could act as.
- Nothing has to be logical. In fact, trying something seemingly illogical, like hanging a rug on the ceiling instead of the floor, is just a way to push your design boundaries.
- It's all worth it. Remember that even if an idea feels impractical, weird, or silly, it's still worth considering (and maybe even trying) because doing so will keep you moving toward a design that feels unique to you.

Ultimately, the "What if?" method isn't about getting things "right." It's about fostering a sense of play and discovery in your design process. You never know where your thoughts will take you until you start asking, "What if . . . ?"

MULTI-SURFACE MURALS

When most people think of a mural, they think of a giant painted piece of art on a wall or building. And while that's a perfectly reasonable thing to do with your walls (and I encourage it), I want you to think beyond the constraints of just putting a mural on a wall. Thinking outside the box—and beyond a room's borders—is how you can really make things more interesting in your home. Because when you think about it, paint doesn't really have boundaries. You can technically paint on nearly every surface you can see in your home. We set the boundaries on where we should and shouldn't paint a mural. What if you stopped yourself from thinking about your home and its surfaces that way? As what "can" and "can't" be painted? What if you instead saw every surface as a possible canvas? We can continue a painting beyond just the designated wall. We can paint over fireplaces, on ceilings, on floors, on wooden decks, on bricks—on just about anything! The benefit of thinking about murals in this boundaryless way is that you can really harness their power. You can use a mural to lead your eye across a room. Or to highlight something you think is really special and otherwise might go unnoticed. You can use one to fill in empty space without having to use objects or buy more things. Or to tie together the color palette of a room.

OVER THE FIREPLACE

When my friend Adrienne was decorating the other side of her duplex house to be a short-term rental, she wanted to create a minimal space without too much clutter so that it would feel modern, clean, and like a refreshing place to relax. But she didn't want the room to feel boring or empty, either. Adrienne thought a mural on the living room's main wall could add a lot of color and warmth to the entire home. In the middle of the wall was a beautiful old fireplace, and I had originally designed a mural to go on the wall around the fireplace. But after sketching out the idea, that design just felt like too much around the fireplace that was so plain. The fireplace surround's natural wood had already been painted over with white paint long ago, so there was no reason to stop us from painting it. So what if I extended the wall mural across the fireplace? The entire room became exciting and unexpected thanks to not being afraid to paint over an architectural feature.

OVER DOORS

Sazerac Stitches is a New Orleans–based company that creates really colorful and whimsical lighting, and they wanted to make sure that when their clients came to their showroom, it was as interesting as their light fixtures are. So they asked for a mural to go on the main room's tall, wooden pocket doors, and they shared a color palette that matched and complemented their lighting lines. As I sketched out what a mural on the doors could look like, I didn't want to feel confined to just the modest surface of the doors themselves. So I sketched out ideas that included painting the doors but *also* going beyond the doors and onto the doorframe and the adjoining walls. What if a mural wasn't constrained to one type of surface? What if I pretended the doors didn't exist and just painted a mural across the entire wall itself? The result is a colorful, graphic mural stretching beyond just the doors, creating a huge, eye-catching art piece across one wall. And as the doors are opened and closed throughout the day, the mural becomes interactive, changing its appearance and the vibe of the whole room. Proof of the power of painting beyond boundaries.

OVER THE EDGE

When my friends Joey and Mark and I were redecorating the basement in their last house, we hung up a fun thrifted art piece in a seating area. The piece was a 1970s-style wavy line that stretched from one side of the canvas to the other. Though it was a fairly large and visually commanding piece, after we hung it, the opposite wall of the room felt too empty. The whole corner of the room just felt like it needed a little bit more. We loved the graphic look of the thrifted art, and we started to wonder what else the artist might have painted if the canvas had been bigger. Would the lines have gotten bigger? Changed colors? Kept going? We wondered what it would look like if *we* extended the artwork beyond the canvas and onto the wall. So we matched the paint colors in the art piece and painted more of the art's line designs on the adjacent wall. It was fun to imagine the painting not having any borders, and it ended up feeling like you were in the painting itself after we were finished.

MATISSE
GALERIE D'ART DE LILLE
EXPOSITION
2-36 Rue Font del Sauix, 59800 Lille, France

OVER THE FRAME

I borrowed Joey and Mark's mural-beyond-the-canvas idea and did a much simpler version in my parents' home in Idaho. It's a perfect example to consider if you're not feeling confident to go big. You can start somewhere really small, like I did with the print I ordered online and framed. I color-matched some of the colors in the print and then used paint to "extend" some of the botanical motifs beyond the print itself. It's just a half circle and a leaf painted on the frame and the wall beside it, but it makes the whole piece more interesting and unexpected. And it's something just about anyone can do. Not everything needs to be overly complicated to be impactful or interesting.

OVER THE FLOOR

Mark and Joey had this little tucked-away room in their attic that had already been painted white from floor to ceiling. It was very small and didn't really have a purpose, but that made it the perfect place to experiment. Since the old wood floors were already a blank canvas, Joey and I worked on creating a mural together. First, we grabbed some pencils and started drawing lines and shapes with no plan at all. We just sketched patterns, allowing our designs to run into each other and happen organically. Once we were satisfied with the pencil designs, we both grabbed paintbrushes and started adding color with paint. As we painted and played, one of us wondered what it would look like if we kept painting, taking the lines and colors of the floor mural up onto the wall . . . and so we did! We both love the result of a last-minute "What if?" decision. It was a small detail that made a big difference.

embrace the unexpected

When Tim and I built the wooden deck in our backyard, it was never a question that we'd have to cover the wood's surface with some substance to protect it. New Orleans weather can be pretty tough on materials like wood, so we knew that to keep the decking safe and good-looking, we'd need to give it a finish.

The traditional route would have been choosing an exterior waterproof stain to seal the wood or perhaps using an exterior paint in a sensible, solid color. But instead of jumping to the first, most expected option, I asked myself, "What if I painted a mural on the deck and seal that instead?"

And so I did, and it's my absolute favorite little outside area to sit and enjoy the nice New Orleans weather.

Designing a beautiful and personal home isn't about trying to be perfect. It's not always doing what's "right." And it certainly shouldn't be trying to only ever do what's "expected." In my opinion, creating a beautiful home is about exploration and playing with ideas. But to *really* let yourself be free to play and have fun in your home, you've got to do something first.

YOU HAVE TO BE WILLING TO TAKE A RISK TO DO THE UNEXPECTED

Worrying that what you're doing is out of the ordinary is one of the biggest obstacles to creating a home that truly feels like *you*. I understand that it's natural to hesitate or even second-guess ideas that don't fall under the classification of "typical." I still question my own ideas sometimes.

But when I catch myself falling into the trap of worrying that I've never seen someone try this or that I might "ruin" something if I play around with a wild idea, I try to channel the kind of creative outlook I had as a kid. Back

then, no idea ever felt too big or too out-there. I didn't question if something was "right"—I just did it. These thoughts were never even on my radar. I was simply creating for the joy of it, experimenting, and figuring things out as I went. And honestly, I think some of the best, most inspired ideas come from that place of fearless creativity, where you're not worried about perfection, judgment, or wasting time.

IF I CONSTANTLY DID THE EXPECTED, THEN THE UNEXPECTED WOULD NEVER HAPPEN

I can't guarantee that every experiment will work out or that there won't be mistakes that need fixing—but the truth is, things can be repainted, stripped, sanded, removed, glued back on, etc. Trial and error is part of the process.

But in the unlikely event that you do something and absolutely hate it, even that's not a failure. It's just a step in your design process toward creating a home that truly fits your personality.

Of course, it's worth sitting with really wild ideas that could actually significantly damage or permanently alter something in your home to make sure it's a risk you want to take. But if you feel the pull to try something really wild, I think you should take the leap. For example, in our kitchen, I decided to paint stripes on our grasscloth wallpaper (see page 103). At the time, I had never seen anyone paint over grasscloth, but I thought it would be interesting. I did run the risk of hating it and then having to pull all the paper down, but in the end, it looked great, and it was worth trying something unexpected.

NEVERMIND

LAYERED GALLERY

Sometimes I play around by asking myself, "What if . . . ?" because I'm bored. When it came to creating a gallery wall in our New Orleans rental apartment bedroom, I just didn't want to do a gallery wall like I'd always done. I'd explored hanging art both squished really close together and with a lot of extra space between the frames. This time, I wanted to do something different. I ran through various scenarios of how to make the gallery wall feel fresh. What if instead of just hanging on one wall, the gallery wrapped onto the neighboring wall? I liked that direction, but the gallery wall still felt too flat. What if I made the gallery wall more dimensional? I started playing by layering the art on top of each other, and I loved it. By using extra-long nails, I was able to hang several pieces in front of others to figuratively and literally make the gallery's wall art pop.

"WHAT IF?" IN THE WILD: KATE PEARCE'S GALLERY WALL

For many of us, a big empty wall is the perfect place for a gallery—a collection of your favorite art pieces. And while a big blank canvas like an empty wall is certainly a place you can hang a gallery, know that it's not the only place. When walls have doors, windows, or other large permanent architectural features, we tend to overlook them as a location for a gallery wall. But doing that could make you miss out on amazing art display possibilities. Designer Kate Pearce, for instance, didn't let the fact that there is a giant window in the middle of her dining room nook's wall prevent her from creating a dreamy gallery wall composition. The window seamlessly fits into her art hanging arrangement, and with its black trim and the addition of some patterned café curtains, the window itself feels like a piece of art.

RUG INSTALLATIONS

Rugs are one of my favorite home decor elements. They add unparalleled amounts of color, pattern, texture, and warmth to your home. And while laying them on the floor under furniture is a great way to use them, it's far from the only place you can decorate with rugs. Rugs can be hung on walls to create striking art pieces that add depth and dimension to your space. They can also be repurposed to upholster furniture, such as benches or headboards, to bring a touch of softness and intricate design. With a little creativity, rugs can transform almost any surface in your home into something unique and eye-catching. Objects do not have to be used how they are intended to be, and these projects are proof.

RUG ON THE CEILING

Our kitchen in Portland had a light fixture I loved, but it felt really small compared to all the other details of the space. I considered installing a round ceiling medallion above the light fixture to add visual weight to the area. Then I looked down at a round jute rug on the floor. I loved the natural texture of the material and the detailed design. It wasn't too physically heavy, either. I thought, *What if I do the opposite of what you would normally do with a rug and put it on the ceiling instead of the floor?* It took screws, nails, and a little trial and error to install the rug on the ceiling, but the result is an unexpected location for a rug that surprisingly works as an unexpected medallion for the light.

RUG ON THE BAR

Placing a rug on our New Orleans rental apartment's kitchen island came about in a similar way that hanging the rug on the ceiling did. I had more rugs than rooms thanks to my habit of picking up things I love while out thrifting and shopping. I wanted to add color, pattern, and texture to my rental apartment's plain kitchen island. I had already painted it once and hung wallpaper, so using a rug felt like the next step in pushing it further. It created a bold look in a fresh way that also added a lot of personality to the room.

RUG ON THE FRIDGE

There's probably not a single surface I haven't considered adding a rug to now that I've seen how great they look in places other than the floor, and one of the latest ways I played around with a rug is in our Winnebago, where I made over the mini fridge. I should state up front that putting a rug on your refrigerator might not be the most practical option. But when you have the chance to play around in a space that's used for only short periods of time, like an RV, I think it's the perfect opportunity to try something a little bit different or weird. I had previously covered our RV's mini fridge with botanical-inspired peel-and-stick wallpaper, but I wanted to add even more texture to the teeny space. So I cut up a color-blocked rug and adhered it to the outside of the fridge, elevating a plain appliance and adding detail in an unusual spot. It's quirky and weird and definitely not for everyone. Just the way I like it.

BEADED BED SKIRT

One of the best things about the "What if?" method is that you can "What if?" nearly every aspect of something. You can wonder not just about an object's material (or what else it could be made from), but you can also wonder about an element's location (or other places it could be located). The perfect example is the beaded skirt I made for the guest room in my parents' house in Idaho. I was looking through a design book featuring 1970s beaded curtains, where strings of beads (usually wooden, but sometimes plastic or bamboo) would be installed in doorways to add a little drama and maybe conceal something behind. I wondered where else a beaded curtain could be used to add interest and hide clutter . . . and thought about the bed with all my college art jammed underneath it, alongside old quilts. Some people use fabric bed skirts to add texture to their bed's design, but I wondered what it might look like if, instead of a fabric skirt, I installed a beaded curtain. But I didn't want to just buy some cheap plastic beaded curtains off the internet; I wanted to push the idea of a beaded curtain even further. What if the beads were extra-large wooden balls? The result is a one-of-a-kind, textured, eye-catching addition to an otherwise plain bed that also functions to hide clutter underneath. And it would have never come to be if I hadn't kept asking myself, "What if . . . ?"

Scalloped headboard

Back in the '90s, my dad crafted this headboard for my bedroom in my parents' house. Considering that it was handmade with love using beautiful wood, it would have been understandable if I'd wanted to keep it as is for the good memories. It has certainly held up well over the years and has a classic design that would fit in any style room. But sometimes I think we worry too much about keeping things in their "original" condition. I think it's okay to let things evolve and change throughout the years. To me, refreshing something that you already own and like is a beautiful way to honor the piece. Give it new life and new energy. That's what I did with the headboard, by cutting out a wavy design along the top, as seen on page 177. I haven't altered the spirit of the original design of the headboard; I've just added a little bit of my own current personality to it. If you have a family heirloom that's worth a lot of money, that you might pass down to your kids, or that you love just the way it is, you can keep it as is. But I want you to feel like you can have the exact home you want, and I give you permission to redo and renew any items that you want.

3D WALL SCULPTURE

Adding dimension to your home, however you can, is one of the fastest ways to create a sophisticated and exciting space. And how you add dimension is limited only by your own perceived boundaries. When I was creating a concept for our living room, I really wanted it to have dimension and flow. The far wall was a blank canvas, and when we first moved in, I splashed color and pattern on it with simple paint murals. And while that added a lot of dimension to the room, I wanted to push the idea even further. And so, I added three-dimensional shapes. Tim and I built shallow boxes out of plywood that we installed on the wall. Over the years, I changed the colors and wove string lights around and behind some of the added shapes. The current iteration of our three-dimensional wall mural is my favorite: I painted a modernist, abstract-inspired large-scale mural of a vase over the wall's wooden additions, creating a slightly disorienting visual display that pulls your eye in and makes a huge statement in the room.

BOHEMIANS

DIY LIGHT

Whenever I go thrifting, I love to focus on the shapes of items . . . not what an item's typical intended use is. When I came across a vintage wooden chip and dip platter and bowl, their function of holding snacks barely crossed my mind. What immediately caught my attention was the circle-atop-a-circle shape. I enjoyed the overall look and feel of the objects—their materiality, their organic curves, and their texture—way more than I considered how they might normally be used. I started to think about how else these beautiful round objects could be used in a home. I wondered what they would look like hanging on a wall and physically held them up in front of me. As I saw them in front of a wall, I was able to envision them not only hanging on the wall as art but also holding a lightbulb and transforming into a light fixture. In fact, adding light into the mix would be the perfect way to highlight the pieces' great shapes and texture. They ended up being the perfect minimalist light for my friends Adrienne and Keith's bedroom.

FROM BOOKCASE TO CONSOLE

Sometimes conceiving of the perfect transformation for something can be as simple as looking at an object, wondering, "What if . . . ?," and turning it on its side. This bookcase of Mark and Joey's had always been used as intended, standing upright and holding items on the shelves. But when the couple moved into their new home, there really wasn't a good spot for it anymore. Still, they didn't want to get rid of the piece. The thing is, they did need a nice long console for their new dining room. I wondered what would happen if we turned the bookcase on its side . . . and it turned out to be the perfect size to act as a dining room console. After we flipped the bookcase on its side, we added a thick piece of wood on the top and sides and spray-painted the entire piece to make it feel cohesive. And voilà—the bookcase became a functional piece in a whole new way.

YOUR TURN

The "What if?" method is about playing around, pushing limits, and asking yourself how you can take projects just a few steps further to see what you can create. It's an invitation to play, experiment, and reimagine what's possible. It's not a step-by-step set of rules that you have to follow. It's me encouraging you to make tiny tweaks, try out unexpected ideas, push yourself a little, and discover a design process that feels liberating and deeply personal for you.

So, take some time now to look around your home. Is there anything that feels like it could be just a little something more? Just for fun—with no obligation to do anything—and for the sake of practice, pick an item or items in your home and start thinking about how you could use them entirely differently. Get wild and have fun.

Maybe you already have something in mind after reading this chapter. Think of the space and ask yourself some "What if?" questions. What if the color/texture/art was on the ceiling? What if you hung the item on the door instead of the wall? What if you used that thing to decorate another piece of furniture instead of having it be a separate object?

Not everything you think of needs to make sense. Not everything you think of even has to be tried. It's the very practice of thinking outside the box that will slowly help you build that muscle of being creative. If nothing is off-limits, then anything is possible.

MINI METHODS & QUICK TRICKS

While I hope that playing around with the three main methods in this book will help you achieve home design results like you've never seen before, you might occasionally be in the mood for something a little more bite-sized. My mini methods and quick tricks are the perfect snack: They are creative tips designed to jump-start your imagination and get your creativity flowing. As with all the methods, you can use them if you're feeling stuck, bored, or simply uninspired and are in the mood to play. Whether you're out thrifting, painting a mural, reupholstering a headboard, or wondering what project to tackle next, these mini methods might offer a bit of design direction.

But while they offer guidance, like all my methods, they aren't meant to be hard-and-fast rules. Use these like all the ideas in this book—to see if they spark your own creativity to create something unique. You can use each one of these mini methods on their own to push beyond a project's perceived boundaries, or you can mix a few when you're feeling extra stuck. And yes, you can even tack a mini method or two on to any of the book's main methods to supercharge your creativity.

Whether you use these mini methods for a big project or something a bit more modest, remember that even the tiniest tweaks can lead to impactful results. And even the smallest mindset shifts can lead you to one-of-a-kind design ideas that help you create a personal home that's meaningful. Most of all, I hope they are little ways you can help yourself think outside of the ways you normally do.

LOOK AT THE SHAPE

I mentioned shape briefly on page 184, but it's such an important part of how I create that I wanted to explain more. The shape of an object is perhaps the most vital thing to look for when you're out thrifting or at estate sales. While it's not *impossible* to alter the shape of something—you can disassemble an item to change its frame, just as you can glue on extra material to make a different form—keeping the shape of something the same and updating its color and finish is much easier. So, if you are on the hunt for shapes instead of finishes, you can always refresh that object in much easier ways if you're starting with a shape you like.

Going to thrift stores that are packed full of eclectic items can be overwhelming, and sometimes it's hard to see through all the visual noise. Instead of trying to train your mind to search for a bunch of different characteristics, just practice looking for shapes that catch your attention first.

When I'm shopping, instead of trying to take everything in at once, I let my eyes quickly scan the shelves to see if the shape of anything, like a nice curvy candlestick or a weird abstract sculpture, grabs my attention. Sometimes I'll see a shape I love and not even know what the item is at first. But if the shape of something is good, it doesn't even matter. I can use the shapely object as intended or reimagine it into something entirely new.

I spotted these huge waffle cubes in the toy section of a thrift store. I loved their size and unique shape. After some brainstorming, I realized that if I added a base and spray-painted them, they would make perfect end tables for our guest room.

DO THE UNEXPECTED OR THE OPPOSITE

Doing something unexpected or the opposite of what you're meant to do with a room or an object can lead to the most playful ideas. We have been told as adults that things are meant to be a certain way or that items can be used only in the way they were intended. I think it's a shame that we sometimes lose our childlike imagination as we grow up. Remember when you were a kid, when a few chairs and a blanket could become a whole pretend "castle"? When I was little, I used to fill ziplock bags full of water and pretend they were waterbeds for my Barbie. It can be hard to tap into that creative mindset of being a kid, when you didn't look at things around you as what they *were* but as what they *could be*. However, one way I try to do that myself is by considering the unexpected application or opposite use of an item.

So, if a rug normally goes on a floor . . . what would it look like on the ceiling? Curtains are usually hung to cover windows, but what if you hung them to cover something else, like an entrance to the hall or room? What if you used sheets as curtains? Nightstands are usually meant to be on either side of your bed, but what if you instead lined them up at the foot of the bed? Outdoor furniture is intended to be used outside, but what if you brought an outdoor chair you love inside?

Designer Rosie Case did that very thing when she brought a metal flower intended to be used as outdoor art inside her home. Yes—the idea of looking at opposites can quite literally be this easy! But while simple, it's proof that reconsidering the intended uses and locations of objects can lead to whimsical additions to your space.

The point is not to live in a home with no table lamps on tables and rugs only on the ceiling rather than the floor—the point is to physically move an object into an "unusual" place to see how it makes you feel. To see if it makes you think about that object or that space in a different way. Doing the "opposite or unexpected" with an object is a way to not only challenge your preconceived notions about things but also help you take objects out of context. So you can stop looking at what things are . . . and start seeing what they could become.

Content creator Gianna Caputo had this knife block that wasn't working for her; the knives were too long and hit the counter. But instead of getting rid of the block, she found a creative and unexpected way to use it by making it a "vase" for dried flowers.

SHOP YOUR OWN SPACE

I have a passion for thrifting and secondhand shopping, not just because I love a deal but also because I believe in being sustainable and reusing or making over things that already exist. And while I'm obviously a huge fan of thrift stores, resale stores, and estate sales, there's another place I shop at frequently: my own space.

I didn't invent the idea of shopping your own space; I'm sure it's something crafty and budget-minded folks have been doing for a very long time. But while it's not a new idea, it's an idea worth championing because it encapsulates so many of the things I find important in design: using what you already have, refreshing your space often, letting your space evolve, and changing things to be the way you want them to be.

If you love to collect items the way I do, then you've got a great amount of potential for change on hand already. Even if your house is not packed full, the simple act of moving things from one room to another can make it feel like you've got a whole new space.

Some of us place an item in a spot in our home and then never move it. It's almost like the longer something stays in one spot, the more you don't notice it *and* the less you care about it. There's nothing inherently wrong with never moving your things around, but it could lead to a home that feels stagnant and lifeless. One remedy is to shop your own space and take an object or a furniture piece from a room it's always been in and move it into a room you've never thought to put it in. After the move, see how it feels. If you like the addition in the new location *and* you had to move something else out of the way to make room for it, then you now have another object or furniture piece you can play with. Try bringing the displaced item to the location of the first object, or try walking around your home with it and see if you can find a new spot for it.

While you can certainly shop your own space when you feel like there's something "missing" in a particular room, you don't have to limit the use of this mini method to when you're looking to fill a void. You can just be bored and grab any art piece, piece of furniture, or object and start moving it to new locations around your home. Not necessarily to find a new home for an object but to see how different items that normally aren't near each other visually interact. It's like mixing different paints together to see what new colors you can make; you're throwing different home elements next to each other to see what kind of visual reactions you get from them.

Whether you're shopping for a specific function or just for fun, none of your changes have to be permanent. As with everything in this book, I'm sharing ways in which I've been able to spark interesting and unusual home decor ideas. And moving things I already have in my home around—literally playing and experimenting—is one of my favorite and most sustainable ways to do so.

Designer Raisa Sandstrom wanted to update the flooring in her foyer and dining room. But she also wanted the flooring to flow from the kitchen into the dining room. After she'd pulled up the wood that was over fifty years old, it felt like a shame to let it go to waste. Shopping her space—using this wood again—was a way to take something from one place in her home and use it somewhere else. So, she removed all the old nails and sanded and resealed the wood, repurposing it as the new backsplash for her kitchen. The new lighter wood could continue on the floor to tie the two rooms together, but the darker wood still had a place in her home, and even in the kitchen where it had once stood. A piece of history preserved.

TAKE A PICTURE

Take a picture to analyze your space whenever you're having trouble figuring out what to do next. I neither know nor understand the science behind this phenomenon, but I do know that sometimes, seeing something in 2D through my camera or phone screen can help me focus in on the space and really see what's "wrong" or missing.

Maybe it has to do with how when I'm sitting in a space, I can find myself distracted by the extra things in my line of sight. Again, I'm not entirely sure why taking a photo helps me, but you could try it and see if it'll help you, too.

I find that when I'm able to see a sort of "flat" image of the space I'm considering, I'm able to more easily see if there's something off balance visually. Or quickly notice when there's a distracting blank spot in the composition. Taking a photo helps me figure out what I need to concentrate on, and it could do the same for you.

BRAINSTORM WITH FRIENDS

I often speak about how important it is for you to trust yourself—to listen to what you like, to know how you want your home to look. And I've written about how hard it can be to do that when we live in a world with so many distractions (and differing opinions) on social media. But while I caution you not to take to heart any criticisms from strangers on the internet, I do encourage you to seek out thoughts from people whose opinions you value.

Sometimes it doesn't matter how many times you look at a spot in your home (with your eyes or your camera), you just can't be sure of a design solution. When all else fails, bring in a trusted friend. It doesn't have to be someone whose style matches yours exactly, but I hope it is someone who shares a love and appreciation for creative and out-of-the-box ideas.

I think the perfect time to brainstorm with a friend is before you've tried anything. If you're out of ideas, or you're really not sure of what direction you should go in, invite a friend, physically or virtually, into your home and see what ideas they have. Their fresh perspective on your home coupled with their appreciation of your creativity may be just the right combination to give you the perfect design idea. Or, at the very least, even if you don't love their ideas, narrowing down the things you don't like might help you more easily figure out what you do like.

It was a brainstorming session that led to this painted faux palm headboard. My brother and sister-in-law in Australia wanted a mural and needed a headboard. After a lot of creative discussions, we came up with the idea (and great money-saving option) of combining a mural and a headboard into one. We skipped the physical headboard and painted one instead.

DO SOMETHING EASY

One of the ways I get my creativity going is by giving myself a small win. And I do that by choosing something easy to do. Sometimes it's the actual starting of a project that feels the most daunting to me. Building motivation momentum by tackling something unrelated but fun can be a way to make yourself feel like you've made progress. By doing something small and easily achievable, like maybe spray-painting a thrifted find such as a vase or candlesticks, can be a little step toward building your confidence to tackle something bigger. Having fun with tiny, easy projects, even if it's just doing a craft you love and know how to do, is like giving yourself a reward for moving forward. And it's the consistent moving forward that could help you get out of a design rut. It helps me shift my mindset from stagnation to productivity because it's a small, easily achievable task that still feels rewarding. The act of transforming something old or plain into something vibrant and unique gives me a sense of accomplishment. It's not just about the object itself—it's about proving to myself that I can take an idea and bring it to life. These small creative victories boost my confidence and make the larger, more complex projects feel less intimidating. They're like stepping stones, reminding me that creativity doesn't have to come in grand, sweeping gestures; sometimes it begins with a single, satisfying step forward.

When I found this vase at a thrift store, it was dark blue, a color that I wasn't interested in, but I liked the shape of the vase. All it took was a can of textured spray paint to transform the piece into something I loved that worked in my space. It was a quick and gratifying project, and it later served as the inspiration for the mural behind it.

START A COLLECTION

I find that it's so much easier when thrifting, shopping at estate sales, or traveling to have a particular item I'm looking for. Every excursion becomes a hunt. Instead of walking into a vintage shop and feeling overwhelmed, you now have something you can search for. Choose an item you really enjoy—maybe it's necklaces, charms, or scarves, or it could be wooden spoons or rolling pins. Whatever you decide on is fine, and you don't even need to know exactly what you'll do with them yet. Once you have a decent amount, you can start thinking about how to use them creatively. Maybe the necklaces become a chandelier accessory. Or the charms are attached to a picture frame or vase. Or the wooden spoons become the cabinet pulls in your kitchen. The best part is that you can take your time; there's no need to go out and buy one thing in bulk online to move a project forward. Sometimes it's the joy of collecting that's half the fun.

A couple of copper mixing bowls from the dump and a copper pan were the start of a unique collection to hang on the trim of these pocket doors belonging to Raisa Sandstrom. If there's a category of object that you find yourself gravitating toward, consider declaring yourself a collector and start looking for examples the next time you're shopping.

YOUR TURN

Whether it's one of the main methods or a mini one, all the ideas in this book are about finding ways to shift your mindset into a more creative direction. They truly are just little exercises to challenge yourself whenever you think you've reached the end of one of your projects or when the well of ideas has dried up. They're also just fun things to do whenever you're bored, if you're anything like me. If you've got an hour or two, I suggest you try all the mini methods in this chapter in one afternoon, just for fun. You don't have to be stuck or have a design dilemma to solve. In fact, trying out these little tips and tricks when you don't really need a solution can be the best way to see which mini method feels most like you. You can try each method out to see which ones get your creative juices flowing the most.

GET OUT AND GET INSPIRED

The mini methods are tiny tweaks to your mindset that you can use—like tools in a kit—anytime you're feeling stuck or uninspired. They're small and easy to do, and can mostly be tackled while you're physically inside your home. The ideas in this chapter differ in that they're not tips to pull out whenever you need inspiration. They're more like lifestyle suggestions to consider in order to constantly be stoking inspiration.

The more open you are to the world—not only looking around and noticing things but also mentally (or perhaps even physically) cataloging them—the bigger a bucket of ideas and inspiration you'll be able to dip into whenever a design dilemma crosses your path. All the methods in the book are processes you can walk through to help you access the creative parts of your brain . . . and the ideas in this chapter are a way of continuously feeding the creative part of your brain so you have fresh ideas to play around with.

You can use any of the ideas in this chapter whenever you need to get out of your space to gain a new perspective. I can reach a point where I've tried all the methods discussed previously and still feel stuck, and that's when I know it's time to get out and get inspired. But if you're able to, consider regularly getting out of your home to gather inspiration.

I find inspiration nearly everywhere, and you can, too. You could be at a museum and find yourself drawn to a piece of art with an interesting color palette. Maybe you can translate that into your home by painting your walls and ceiling with this unusual combo of colors inspired directly by art. Or maybe it's the shape of a flower or the way a meal was plated at a restaurant that will inspire you. Maybe the texture of the bark on a tree will catch your eye, or the way clothing is layered on a mannequin in the window of a chic shop.

Sometimes just getting out to the thrift store can inspire new ideas or projects that you didn't even plan or see coming. That's what's so fun about the thrift store; you never know what's going to happen. But just going there with an open mind, keeping your eyes open for interesting objects that you're drawn to, and then considering how you can use them in an unexpected way or transform them to suit you better is always great practice for building your design muscles. You don't need to feel pressure to find something every time because, in reality, you probably won't. But that's the exciting part about thrifting: For all the times you don't find something, all it takes is one great find to make it all worth it.

Looking beyond the internet and your own home can be vital for finding the ideas that will inspire you. Not so you can copy exactly what you see out in the world (though that certainly is an option), but so you can allow the ideas you see to simmer in your mind and be translated into your own special style.

And know that none of these ideas has to cost a lot of (or any) money. Most museums have free days when you can visit their exhibits. You don't have to stay at a hotel or eat at a restaurant to get a glimpse of their public areas. It costs nothing to explore a city and look at the architecture or nature around you. And libraries and secondhand stores have lots of vintage design books just waiting to be leafed through for ideas.

I know that I'm so privileged to have been able to travel to some of the places I've visited. And I recognize that not everyone might be able to do that. I'll always advocate for traveling whenever it's possible because it's been such a big influence on my style. But you don't have to spend a ton of money accessing far-flung places to find inspiration. When possible, be immersed wherever you are and pay attention to the beauty you can find around you.

VISIT GORGEOUS PUBLIC SPACES

Getting out there and appreciating different styles of design, even if they're not to your particular taste, can be so important. When you stick to the same sources of inspiration, you'll find yourself able to come up with only the same sorts of ideas. By observing what's around you, you open up your mind to possibilities you may not have been able to think of by yourself.

My favorite way to get out and get inspired is by physically experiencing the designs of public spaces. Hotel lobbies and chic restaurants are definitely high on my list when it comes to soaking up good design, but there are a surprising number of public places available to you to walk in and get immersed.

Search online and find out if your city or town has a historic neighborhood or district, and head over there. Whether the architecture is residential or commercial, take the time while you're exploring to really examine the design details you can see from the sidewalk. Pay attention to the way the windows are shaped on buildings or how ornamented things like railings, trim, molding, and tilework are. Do the doors have weathered patinas? What kind of patterns are made by any bricks? Do the exterior color palettes make your heart skip a beat?

You can also often poke around the public areas of university and college campuses, which often have an array of traditional and modern architectural styles. Look for the same sorts of design details and notice how they compare and contrast with each other, too.

Cathedrals, churches, mosques, temples, and other kinds of religious buildings are sometimes open to the public, and as long as you are respectful, slowly and quietly taking in design details as an appreciator of architecture is usually welcome. Libraries, art galleries, and history museums are usually packed with design inspiration inside and out, and entry fees aren't always required.

A city's public art features, such as murals, sculptures, and statues, are often free to view and can offer surprising inspiration. But don't overlook public features that could offer artistic inspiration as well, like fountains, streetlamps, and park benches. There's inspiration everywhere if you take the time to seek it out.

When you're getting out and looking for inspiration, you might find an interesting color palette you never considered before or a pattern that you could use in an unexpected way. Sometimes just being surrounded by good design is enough to get your brain feeling creative, and that's the first step. When I'm immersed in beautiful spaces, it's an endorphin rush.

The ceiling of our guest room was inspired by the parquet flooring of a hotel lobby, reimagined with an interesting color palette. You never know where your next source of inspiration could be found.

LOOK THROUGH VINTAGE DESIGN BOOKS

I love looking to the past for inspiration, and old design books are one of the best places to find ideas. Public libraries often have plenty of older books on the shelves, plus you can almost always find a great design book at a thrift store or an estate sale. Honestly, I pick up and take home most vintage design books I come across (as long as they're reasonably priced). Even if the style looks wildly different from my own, I know there could be some inspiration in the pages. A book full of 1990s floral prints could hide a creative way to display art I've never thought of before. A book that focuses only on luxurious Art Deco–style homes from the 1920s could have a pattern or texture that's perfect for some project I'm working on.

I don't believe that, at this point, there are really any brand-new ideas anymore. Rather, I think most ideas are old ones reimagined. So when I'm looking through these vintage design books, I'm not looking for exact elements to copy. I'm flipping through the pages to see what catches my eye, and then I think about how I can take that concept or nugget of an idea and make it new for me.

The grid I painted on a wall in the primary bedroom of our New Orleans house (see page 113) is based on a graphic pattern on the floor of an amazing room from the '70s or '80s that I spotted in a vintage design book. I thought it would make such a cool statement on a wall instead.

NOTICE NATURE'S PALETTE

Some of the best inspiration is right outside your door. While visiting public parks, botanical gardens, and nature preserves is an amazing way to get out there and be inspired by nature, you don't actually have to go on a hike to mine the natural beauty that is all around us. I believe that some of the most beautiful ideas can come from paying attention to the simple natural elements that surround us every day.

Even if you live in a city, there's always a bit of nature to find inspiration in, whether it is the color of the leaves on the trees or the texture of the trees' bark, the dramatic hues of sunrise or sunset, or even just the shape of the clouds. Inspiration is everywhere. Maybe it's the way a weed's green color contrasts with the concrete as it pokes itself out of the sidewalk.

The kinds of colors, textures, patterns, and designs that you can find in nature will always be a timeless addition to your home, no matter how you interpret them and bring them into your space. By observing the landscape around you (no matter how natural it might be), you have an endless source of ideas. Inspiration truly can be found anywhere—if we take the time to look for it, notice how it makes us feel, and then find a way to bring it into our home. Even gazing outside your window can reveal tons of potential inspiration.

You can take literal inspiration from nature like I did in this home of Amanda Sonneborn in Park City, Utah, where I painted oversized wildflowers on the walls.

LOOK AT OTHER CREATIVE FIELDS

Stick to just the obvious forms of inspiration when it comes to design—like other interiors, art, or even nature—and you might be missing out on other incredible ways to find ideas. The truth is, there are shapes and colors to be found everywhere. The patterns in handmade quilts. The curves or material play in jewelry. Even food and cooking can hold inspiration for your home.

For example, when looking through a cookbook one day, I found myself drawn to and really appreciating the look of braided pretzels. There was something about their shape and size that reminded me of cabinet pulls, for some reason. So then I thought, why couldn't they be just that? Every year for Christmas, my mom makes ornaments out of homemade salt dough, and I realized I could make nonedible pretzel-like creations using the same dough recipe. After braiding the dough in a similar style to the one I saw in the cookbook to create the pulls, I baked them in the oven to harden them, then, after they cooled, spray-painted them and gave them a protective clear coat. When they were dry, I glued them to wooden bases and then screwed them onto our RV cupboards for pretzel-inspired handles. Inspiration from food translated into home design.

repainting

In addition to moving existing elements in your home around, it's also nice to refresh something you already own. And there's absolutely no limit to how many times you can refresh or remodel something, either. You can rescue a secondhand piece of furniture or art, give it a full refresh, and then paint over it just as many times as you want after that. You can make it look different over and over again. There are no rules about how many times you can play with something.

I say this because sometimes I think that along the way, some of us got the idea that you can change something only once. Whether that means remodeling a kitchen, reupholstering a headboard, or even altering a painting we've made ourselves. Whether you love your makeover or are just okay with it, somehow, you feel as if that effort or energy will be wasted if you try something new.

That's just not true. You can update anything in your home anytime you'd like for any reason, no matter how recently you've updated it. You can hate the result or just not be sure you love it. But the point is, you can put as much effort as you like into editing it until it's exactly what you want . . . until you're ready to update it again. You can change the things around you as many times as you are inspired to when you are out exploring the world. Every new inspiration can be a new spark for updating something.

The art in my kitchen/dining room is a perfect example. I made this large art piece out of plyboard and have repainted it at least four times. There was no rhyme or reason to what I painted on the plyboard originally . . . just ideas or colors that I had been inspired by at the time. Each time I changed the art, I'd live with it for a while—a week or a few months—and if it still wasn't feeling great, I just painted something else. Eventually, I landed on a simple pink and red shape, which has lasted quite some time now. Instead of buying a new piece of art every single time my design style evolves, I just paint over the plywood art piece until I like what I see.

TRAVEL

When you travel, you get the privilege of soaking up inspiration from all the different elements of a different place and culture, from the food to clothing, architecture, design, and so much more. A recent trip to Morocco left me bursting with ideas from all the colors, patterns, and textures I saw. The vibrant color palette of a street in a small town inspired the colors of this mural in the home of Amanda Sonneborn.

GO THRIFTING

Sometimes going to a thrift store or visiting an estate sale can trigger a new project you could have never seen coming. That's what's so exciting about thrifting; you never know what you'll come home with. DIYer Lowe Saddler found a horse statue and a ceramic candle warmer at her local thrift store, which inspired her to combine the two and make a lamp.

YOUR TURN

The secret of how a room gets to the next level is in the details. Like an unexpected finish on a doorknob or a colorful painted edge of a piece of furniture. Or even tassels on the corner of a throw pillow. These and similarly small design details don't seem all that impactful on their own. But don't be fooled by their size; the power lies in how you layer them into your home one by one. I believe that the slow accumulation of small design details is what can truly make a home feel personal and one of a kind.

Because of their nature, small design detail updates can be easy to make with little money or time. And because incorporating a small design detail doesn't usually involve a huge design decision, it can be the perfect place to begin for intrepid or not-sure-where-to-start designers.

In order to start creating a home full of personal details, start gathering inspiration today. Look at all the small details around you next time you're away from your home. Give yourself permission to notice elements that make you curious. Practice taking notes, physical or mental, of the things that have grabbed your attention. You don't even have to know what it is you like about something (or even how you will translate that inspiration into your own home). When you find yourself drawn to something—the way a flower's petals are shaped, the color palette of a painting, the way a pastry crust's texture feels—take a photo (if photographs are allowed where you are), jot down thoughts in a notebook, or a make a mental note of the element that has piqued your interest.

Observe and catalog. Then, the next time you're feeling inspired, try playing around to see if there's a way to incorporate some small design details you come across in your home. Or better yet, see if there's a way you can *reinterpret* that small detail in your own magical way.

Always be absorbing inspiration whenever you can. And remember that there's simply no time limit on finding a way to incorporate an inspiring detail you've seen with your own eyes (or felt with your own hands). It can be something you saw years ago or something you saw just yesterday. There are also no limits on how many times you can reference the same element for inspiration. Paint every room in your home the same handful of colors you saw in one painting in a museum if that's truly what you love and want to do.

be yourself

If there's one takeaway I hope you carry with you from this book, it's this: Don't be afraid to be yourself. Whether your home features every color of the rainbow or is completely white from floor to ceiling, what truly matters is that you create a home that looks and feels like you.

Why? Because I truly believe that you can be your best, most creative self when you're surrounded by design choices that match your personality and make you feel excitement and contentment.

In today's ultra-connected world, it can feel like everyone has an opinion about your home decor choices. Whether it's followers on social media or friends, family, neighbors, or even the tradespeople working on your home, there are plenty of people who might have thoughts about what color you painted your ceiling, what tiles you chose, or what kind of art you're displaying on your walls. But even the most talented and popular designer on the planet couldn't create a space that pleases *everyone*. The truth is that design is personal. Why try to satisfy anyone other than yourself? Instead, focus on pleasing yourself and the people who share your home with you.

When you free yourself from the need to please others, you unlock a world of creative possibilities for your home. Without worrying about other people's judgment, you can explore, experiment, and follow your own instincts. And by not seeking approval from the outside world, you get to look for it in the most important place: inside yourself. Instead of designing from a place of fear, you'll find yourself designing fearlessly.

Second-guessing yourself is one of the biggest things that can get in the way of creating a space that's uniquely you. Worse, it can prevent you from ever starting. If something sparks joy

DO NOT TURN
TURN
POP CORN
POP CORN

or curiosity in you—be it a piece of furniture, a bold color, or an unusual decorative element—embrace it. Don't worry if it seems odd to someone else; if you love it, it belongs in your home. Be proud of it.

Designing your home is about feeding the creativity inside you. It's about creating an environment that not only tells your story but also brings you joy every single day. If you love something, don't hold back—go all in.

I encourage you to approach your home with a spirit of playfulness and curiosity. Experiment, explore, and uncover what makes you feel truly at home. By embracing your own creativity and staying true to yourself, you're not just decorating—you're crafting a space that celebrates who you are. And that, above all else, is what makes a home special.

Designer Gladys Tay's home is full of unique and unusual items, making it stand out from the rest. A perfect example of being true to yourself and making your home really reflect you and what brings you joy.

Alka-Seltzer
SPAIN—A HISTORY IN ART
HISTORY OF MODERN ART
NOMA
Coca-Cola
Trademarks ®
SAVINGS 101
SKECHERS

resources

I suggest that you always visit your local thrift/vintage/repurpose store first before buying anything new. You'd be surprised at the amazing things you can find for a great deal if you have time to look around. You can search for local estate sales in your area and find gently used gems that way, too. And be sure to look through Facebook Marketplace, buy-nothing groups, and other local online marketplaces for secondhand finds.

MY FAVORITE THRIFT/ VINTAGE STORES IN NEW ORLEANS

Consign Consign
Floor 13
The Green Project
Merchant House
Red White & Blue
ReStore
River Road Flea Market
The Salvation Army

MY FAVORITE INSTAGRAM ACCOUNTS FOR VINTAGE OR HANDMADE ART, FURNITURE, AND DECOR

@ameliatarbet
@carefullypicked
@cedricsmithstudio
@fabiusgrange
@gillianbryce
@groovythicket
@loftandthought
@6thanddetroit
@s.kayne.designs
@ummmsmile

MY FAVORITE NON-THRIFT SHOPPING SOURCES

Of course, you can't always find exactly what you need secondhand; I have a number of places I shop when I need something new. These are some of my favorite brands:

BEDDING

Cultiver
Kip&Co
Schoolhouse
Trek Light

CURTAINS

Calico Corners
Tonic Living

FURNITURE

AllModern
CB2
Crate & Barrel
Kardiel
Lulu and Georgia
Nadeau

LIGHTING

Anthropologie
Gallery L7
Hudson Valley Lighting
Sazerac Stitches

MATTRESSES

Brentwood Home

PAINT AND ART SUPPLIES

Behr paint
Posca markers
Wooster pro 2-inch thin angled brushes

RUGS

Annie Selke
Enkay
Lulu and Georgia
Rich Class Decor
Swoon Rugs
Voyage Living

WALLPAPER

Pacific Designs
Rebel Walls
Sarah + Ruby
Scout and Nimble

acknowledgments

I still can't believe I have a book. Is this real? After almost three years of working on this and a lifetime of dreaming up ideas, it's truly gratifying to see it all come together here. Of course I never could have done this alone.

Enormous thanks to Tim, who has far more patience and attention to detail than I ever will and helped me make all my wild creations reality. Thank you for your creativity and support. I love you. Wherever we go and whatever space we create will always be perfect because you and Bo are in it.

To my parents, who always said I could do anything and constantly boosted me, giving me the confidence to be myself.

To Adrienne Breaux. Your words are brilliant, and your ability to not only read my mind but also help create the core ideas of this book is what made it all come together. So. Many. Words. We did it!

And of course to my community on Instagram. Who knew that an app could hold such weight in a person's life. I don't think any of this would have been possible without your ongoing support. Thank you!

WHAT
DO
I
DESIRE

Clarkson Potter/Publishers
An imprint of the Crown Publishing Group
A division of Penguin Random House LLC
1745 Broadway
New York, NY 10019
clarksonpotter.com
penguinrandomhouse.com

Library of Congress Cataloging-in-Publication Data
Names: Kamarul, Liz author http://id.loc.gov/authorities/names/n2025010594
Title: Free style: unlock creative home designs / Liz Kamarul with Adrienne Breaux; photographs by Liz Kamarul.
Description: New York: Clarkson Potter/Publishers, [2026] | Identifiers: LCCN 2025009640 (print) | LCCN 2025009641 (ebook) | ISBN 9798217033713 hardcover | ISBN 9798217033720 ebook Subjects: LCSH: Interior decoration http://id.loc.gov/authorities/subjects/sh85067272
Classification: LCC NK2115 .K2595 2026 (print) | LCC NK2115 (ebook) | DDC 747—dc23/eng/20250625
LC record available at https://lccn.loc.gov/2025009640
LC ebook record available at https://lccn.loc.gov/2025009641

ISBN 979-8-217-03371-3
Ebook ISBN 979-8-217-03372-0

Editor: Deanne Katz
Designer: Stephanie Huntwork
Production editor: Patricia Shaw
Production: Kim Tyner
Compositor: Merri Ann Morrell
Copy editor: Sibylle Kazeroid | Proofreaders: Nicole Ramirez, Navorn Johnson
Publicist: Lauren Chung | Marketer: Stephanie Davis

Manufactured in China

10 9 8 7 6 5 4 3 2 1

First Edition

The authorized representative in the EU for product safety and compliance is Penguin Random House Ireland, Morrison Chambers, 32 Nassau Street, Dublin D02 YH68, Ireland, https://eu-contact.penguin.ie.